NEW APPROACHES TO ELEMENTARY MUSIC EDUCATION

Rebecca Herrold
San Jose State University

PRENTICE-HALL, INC., ENGLEWOOD CLIFFS, NEW JERSEY 07632

Library of Congress Cataloging in Publication Data

HERROLD, REBECCA. *(date)*
    New approaches to elementary music education.

    Bibliography: p. 207
    Includes indexes.
        1. School music—Instruction and study. I. Title.
MT930.H59 1983   327.8′7   83-9746
ISBN 0-13-611723-6

Editorial/production supervision and
    interior design: Dan Mausner
Cover design: George Cornell
Manufacturing buyer: Raymond Keating

Printed in the United States of America

10 9 8 7 6 5 4

0-13-611723-6

PRENTICE-HALL INTERNATIONAL, INC., *London*
PRENTICE-HALL OF AUSTRALIA PTY. LIMITED, *Sydney*
EDITORA PRENTICE-HALL DO BRASIL, LTDA., *Rio de Janeiro*
PRENTICE-HALL CANADA INC., *Toronto*
PRENTICE-HALL OF INDIA PRIVATE LIMITED, *New Delhi*
PRENTICE-HALL OF JAPAN, INC., *Tokyo*
PRENTICE-HALL OF SOUTHEAST ASIA PTE. LTD., *Singapore*
WHITEHALL BOOKS LIMITED, *Wellington, New Zealand*

Contents

Verses in duple meter.

Preface

This text has been prepared for elementary music methods classes at the college level and will be useful for inservice teachers' workshops and curriculum planners. It is intended to help prospective classroom teachers develop basic skills in music fundamentals through participation in an integrated, sequential curriculum and the planning and presentation of lessons for the classroom. Prerequisite music courses are helpful, but not necessary. The spiral organization of materials and methods makes it possible for the nonmusician or teacher with little previous musical experience to acquire the knowledge needed to bring music to elementary school children on a daily, or at least frequent, basis.

In schools where music specialists visit the classrooms occasionally, classroom teachers who have personally experienced the vital aspects of the music curriculum are able to contribute significantly to the overall success of the general music program. However, in many schools general music is the responsibility of the classroom teacher. Here it is essential that the teacher be prepared to share the joy of music with young people in ways that allow growth in the areas of musical response and music literacy. This is best achieved through a performance-oriented environment in which children play many roles, including those of singer, accompanist, dancer, conductor, and arranger-composer. For children fortunate enough to experience music in these ways, music is not something that happens *to* them. It becomes something they can do too and it is not reserved for a special few.

The rationale for the text is also based on the author's observation that despite the pedagogical advances in the elementary music field during the past decade, there is frequently little follow-through from the college methods class to the teaching strategies practiced in the elementary classroom. School music programs are strengthened by clear structure and definable goals, including the intent to preserve the rich folk music heritage which is threatened with extinction. Teachers need an awareness that children acquire musical skills as readily as mathematical or literary ones if given an opportunity to do so through a curriculum organized with specific conceptual steps to achievement.

Therefore, the aim of the author is to present a college text and elementary teacher's guide which simultaneously accomplishes several important goals and addresses evident problems in the musical preparation of teachers. Elements of this program include

1. An overall plan that frees the college methods professor from the necessity of searching through many sources for skill-building exercises and assignments at a given level of achievement.
2. The use of the American folk song heritage as basic material for teaching elementary music skills.
3. A spiral organization of curriculum which enables the prospective teacher to study the text as a student in the college classroom and continue its application in the elementary school.
4. Information regarding the impact of modern technology on the elementary classroom and its value to the music teacher.

Curwen hand signs, durational and melodic syllables, accompaniments for pitched mallet instruments, and attention to the study of musicianship through movement are presented with song materials. Although these features are commonly associated with the Kodaly Singing School, the Orff Schulwerk, and Dalcroze eurhythmics methodologies, the overall approach is eclectic with no single prevailing ideology. The author assumes that the methods instructor will acquaint students with the various state-adopted textbooks in the basal series, listening lessons, and elementary introduction to world musics.

The text is organized in an integrated style so that prospective teachers are introduced to elementary songs and activities in the same order as is proposed for schoolchildren. There are no separate sections on playing instruments, reading notation, or elements of music. Rather, each of the four principal sections (Parts 2, 3, 4, and 5) brings all of these into the classroom simultaneously. This assures that a variety of experiences, including those in the cognitive, affective, and motor domains, will be part of the teacher's background.

The songs are the basis for the key divisions in the materials, and they are grouped according to their pentatonic or diatonic orientation. The rhythmic simplicity of some of the diatonic materials makes it feasible to use them as rote songs or for call-and-response activity earlier than their placement in the text implies.

Assignments in reading, writing, and ear-training practice are included throughout the text for the methods class. These are intended to serve as model lessons from which prospective teachers can develop their own classroom materials.

Prose is deliberately kept to a minimum: *the emphasis here is on active student participation.* Model lessons should be presented by the instructor and then by the students. Where possible, work with classes of children provides the most beneficial experience of all.

R.H.

Part 1

Instructional Objectives for the Music Class

The teacher who knows what he or she should accomplish and who takes sufficient time to plan carefully is already well on the way to success. Work will be enjoyable and relieved of much of the stress inherent in a demanding occupation as long as specific objectives are in mind each day and materials and supplies are ready when needed. The organized teacher accomplishes much more with less effort than would be necessary in an unstructured environment, and ultimately will be the teacher who loves his or her work and students. An investment in planning pays rich dividends!

Long-range goals for the elementary music class must be developed through the efforts of the key personnel involved in the teaching. These may include a music supervisor, music specialist, and classroom teachers. In schools where classroom teachers must take full responsibility for the general music program, a person in the school who has some musical background may assist in the planning. Junior high school general, vocal, and instrumental music teachers may be of considerable help in defining expected levels of classroom achievement in music so that students can successfully participate in music activities when they leave the elementary level.

The basic question to consider when confronted with the task of stating objectives for a year, a month, or a day is this: What will the students be able to do as a result of our mutual efforts that they couldn't do before? Do we want them to be able to read music? To respond to many types of musics? To accompany themselves on folk instruments? To move to music? To be able to sing? To know a large number of songs for group singing that they will carry with them throughout life? To be able to compose music? To harmonize a tune?

Certainly all of the above are worthy goals for general elementary classroom music teachers. But they are broad and their place in the six or seven years of a child's elementary school life is unclear. They need to be broken down into manageable parts. This can be done more readily if the following parameters are considered:

1. How much time will be devoted to music instruction?
2. What are the most important things to include in a child's musical experiences considering the time available?
3. What goals are attainable when the teacher's background and the motivation of the community are considered?
4. What materials and resources are available?

Since these factors determine the size and scope of the elementary music program and differ markedly from place to place, it is difficult to establish specific goals for adoption by everyone. The existence of many philosophies regarding curriculum and methodology affects goal development, too. Some educators believe children should sing only folk and art songs, while others would include music from the pop and commercial areas. Some advocate music reading, while others believe this gets in the way of the natural aesthetic response. Some seldom or never use instruments to accompany children's singing, while others develop whole programs around classroom instruments.

Some principal aims are common to all: above all, we want children to enjoy and respond to music, to be able to create and recreate it, and to develop some awareness of the elements of the discipline. Admittedly, these goals can be met in a variety of ways.

Teachers should develop curricular objectives which include activities they themselves enjoy, for the most important musical influence on a child may not be a decision about what is taught when, but the reaction of the teacher to the music. The teacher's enjoyment is sensed by children, and should result in a high degree of class motivation for the singing, creating, movement, or performing that is the activity at hand.

The Primary Years

The objectives stated in this section are correlated to Parts 2 and 3 in this text and are general rather than specific. They tell you what students will be able to do as a result of curriculum developed around these sections, but do not impose limitations on the materials one may add. These objectives are categorized by type of activity, and planners are encouraged to use something from each category if limited by time constraints.

A. *Chanting, Call-and-Response:* The student will
  1. Imitate teacher-led chants and verses with changes in volume, pitch, and tempo.
  2. Respond to chanted or sung questions.
  3. Participate in chanting a repertoire of verses which features duple meter and the rhythms associated with beginning-level songs and movement.
  4. Chant verses in several ways: two or more verses performed simultaneously by the class groups; small group answered by large group; soloist with large group.
B. *Singing:* The student will
  1. Join in group singing of songs learned by rote and drawn principally from the folk repertoire of the native country.
  2. Match tones with the teacher when receiving help in class.
  3. Show correct posture and breathing habits.
C. *Accompanying:* The student will
  1. Participate in performing simple clapped *ostinati* (repeated) patterns with the songs.
  2. Perform simple hand drum and rhythm instrument ostinati.
  3. Perform simple ostinati and *bordun* patterns on xylophones and tone bars. (See Glossary.)
  4. Strum the autoharp in a rhythmic pattern previously clapped or played on rhythm instruments.
D. *Moving:* The student will
  1. Imitate teacher-led echo clapping, stamping, *patschen* (thigh slapping), and snapping.
  2. Step to the beat of a song.

   3. Clap the rhythm of a song.
   4. Step to the beat and clap the rhythm of the song while thinking through its melody and rhythm.
   5. Participate in circle dances.
   6. Respond in movement exercises and games to changes in volume, pitch, and tempo.
   7. Mirror the teacher in preparatory motions for mallet instrument playing.
E. *Reading and Writing:* The student will
   1. Locate staff placement for notes on the *pentatonic scale (sol, mi, la, do, re)* when shown the location of *do.*
   2. Respond in singing to the Curwen hand signs for the syllables indicated above.
   3. Participate with the class in melodic dictation lessons with intervals drawn from songs used for teaching reading.
   4. Respond in movement and durational syllables to duple meter notation, including quarter, eighth, half, dotted half, and sixteenth note patterns; quarter, eighth, and half rests.
   5. Read short instrumental pieces for rhythm instruments.
   6. Identify like and different measures.
   7. Identify a song previously studied by hearing or reading its melody and rhythm.
F. *Listening:* The student will
   1. Listen to live music: the teacher, the class, small groups, soloists, classroom accompaniments, guest instrumentalists and vocalists.
   2. Respond to the mood of the music with a growing vocabulary, for example ''sad,'' ''happy,'' ''rushing,'' ''tired,'' etc.
   3. Identify fast-slow tempos, high-low sounds, dynamic changes (loud-soft).

The Intermediate Years

The following activities are added to those indicated for the primary years. Review, including that of beginning concepts, is necessary for continued growth. Each class session should include a review lesson. New ideas and concepts should be introduced within a context of previously studied material whenever possible.

A. *Chanting:* The student will
   1. Participate in chanting verses in compound meter.
   2. Chant with attention to legato, staccato, rubato, fermata, and dynamic contrasts. (See glossary.)
   3. Suggest various ways to perform verses and rhymes.
   4. Perform a solo part in a chant.
B. *Singing:* The student will
   1. Participate in group singing of songs from the folk song repertoire and the basal series.
   2. Sing descants, second parts, canons, and rounds.
   3. Sing in groups with and without accompaniments.
   4. Sing solo measures or lines.
C. *Accompanying:* The student will
   1. Strum two- and three-chord autoharp accompaniments guided by charts which indicate rhythms and chord changes.
   2. Strum simple guitar accompaniments in easy keys, using a *capo* where necessary.
   3. Create ostinato and bordun patterns for the *Orff instrumentarium* (See glossary).
   4. Suggest and perform bodily movement accompaniments that are derived from the beat and rhythm of a song.
   5. Perform resonator bell accompaniments which include two or three chords.
D. *Moving:* The student will
   1. Extend echo-clapping and echo-moving exercises to include eight measures in duple meter.
   2. Participate in two-circle and parallel-line dances.

3. Respond in movement to sounds (drum or piano) that indicate syncopation and dotted rhythms.

4. Suggest and perform movement activities to accompany songs; suggest dance steps in an appropriate meter and tempo for a song.

5. Conduct two- and four-beat patterns.

E. *Reading and Writing:* The student will

1. Locate staff placement for notes in the *extended pentaton* (*la,*, *sol,*, *do′*, *re′*, *mi′*).

2. Respond in singing to the Curwen hand signs for the syllables indicated above.

3. Participate with the class in melodic dictation lessons with intervals drawn from new songs used to teach reading.

4. Respond in movement and durational syllables to $\frac{3}{4}$ and $\frac{6}{8}$ patterns and the corresponding notation for each.

5. Read syncopated patterns.

6. Complete a short composition for rhythm instruments.

7. Mark like and different phrases in a song.

8. Take rhythmic dictation, including eighth and sixteenth note combinations.

F. *Listening:* The student will

1. Identify specific instruments, families of instruments, and vocal sounds both recorded and live.

2. Identify the melodic contour and metrical organization of the music.

3. Listen to a variety of musical styles—classical, jazz, folk, country, world musics.

4. Build a musical vocabulary to assist in identification of styles, composers' names, and theoretical concepts.

The Upper Grades

Review of primary and intermediate level concepts provides a solid foundation on which these more advanced skills can be built.

A. *Chanting:* The student will

1. Participate in chanting verses in mixed meter and irregular meters.

2. Chant verses in canon style and as rondos.

3. Create chants from familiar names, advertisements, cheers, and greetings.

4. Chant verses while creating accompaniments on rhythm instruments.

B. *Singing:* The student will

1. Participate in group singing of unison and two- and three-part songs from the folk song repertoire and the basal series.

2. Harmonize songs in thirds and sixths.

3. Harmonize songs with vocal accompaniments on **I, IV,** and **V₇** chords.

4. Sing solo phrases.

C. *Accompanying:* The student will

1. Play countermelodies for songs on the soprano recorder.

2. Perform in the Orff instrumentarium song accompaniments which include tonic-dominant harmonies and modes.

3. Locate **I** and **V₇** chords on the piano and perform simple accompaniments for selected songs.

4. Perform autoharp and guitar accompaniments from song scores which indicate chord changes.

D. *Moving:* The student will

1. Indicate through expressive movement

a. changes in meter (as performed on drum or piano by the instructor)

b. fast-slow tempi; loud-soft dynamics

c. phrases and cadences

d. monophony and polyphony

e. major-minor shifts

f. sound/silence

    2. Participate in beginning square dances.

    3. Lead the group in echo-movement in duple, compound, or triple meter keeping a steady beat.

E. *Reading and Writing:* The student will

    1. Locate staff placement for the notes indicated by the syllables *fa, ti,* and *ti'.*

    2. Respond in singing to the Curwen hand signs for the syllables indicated above.

    3. Sight-read melodies and excerpts from melodies using sol-fa or numbers.

    4. Compose a song's melody when given lyrics, the rhythm of the lyrics, measures, and the placement of *do.*

    5. Locate whole and half steps on the keyboard.

    6. Write major and minor scales that correspond to the song repertoire.

    7. Take rhythmic dictation, including irregular meters.

F. *Listening:* The student will

    1. Listen to a varied repertoire and identify selected works by genre, name, and composer.

    2. Describe a recording or live performance with a *musical* vocabulary ("rondo," "pianissimo," "English horn," etc.)

    3. Identify major, minor, and modal organization.

    4. Identify mixed and irregular meters and syncopations.

Part 2

Foundations for Music Learning

Music for young children should be of the best quality and provide opportunities for direct involvement through a variety of experiences. The folk music of the child's native country includes a repertoire of songs that provides a direct route to music learning. Many of the songs are pentatonic, in the rhythm of natural movement, and made up of intervals suitable for a child's vocal capabilities. And because folk music influences the composers of art music, children who have experienced a basic core of music that is derived from their native language develop a musicality that allows them to expand their appreciation to include more complex forms and styles.

At the heart of the primary years' curriculum is unaccompanied singing of question-and-answer songs improvised by the teacher and call-and-response songs from the folk repertoire. The descending minor third, the "natural chant" of children, is a good beginning for the singing class. Verses and songs sung on this interval allow children to participate comfortably, for they hear that interval many times throughout early childhood. Mothers call to children on the minor third, and it is universally found in children's games. Speech patterns, verses, rhymes, and jingles chanted with attention to musical qualities inherent in the native language further enhance the program.

Percussion instruments introduced at this level include rhythm sticks, drums, claves, triangles, wood blocks, sleigh bells, and tambourines. They are used to strengthen the child's perception of the rhythmic features of the chants and songs—first the rhythm of the words, then the beats and offbeats. Echo-clapping and question-and-answer movement on patterns derived from the verses and songs can be transferred to instruments, thereby providing initial experiences in improvisation.

Mallet instruments with removable bars include the glockenspiel, xylophone, and metallophone, all used in the ensemble developed for children by the pedagogue-composer, Carl Orff. These instruments give children an opportunity to perform their own accompaniments on repeated patterns without fear of hitting "wrong" notes. They are appropriate for early experiences because they do not overwhelm young voices, and can be used for beginning work in rhythmic and melodic improvisation.

Movement activities include stepping, swaying, and clapping to the beat. Stationary circle groups are effective for "follow-the-leader" movements to the songs and acting out the lyrics. While the teacher performs with a drum or at the keyboard, children can employ free-response motions to indicate changes in pitch, tempo, dynamics, accent placement, and timbre.

Reading and writing skills are developed from the song repertoire. Here it is important for the teacher to remember that experience must precede reading. Singing, playing, and movement build reading readiness. The songs in Part 2 are learned by rote first; then the procedure for teaching reading are followed.

For the teacher of elementary music, patience is essential; the teacher may tire of repeated work with pentatonic songs and want to move forward before the children have acquired a solid foundation. Mastery of each step is the key to success.

Call-and-Response Songs

Call-and-response activity should be frequently included in the music class. It gives children the opportunity to hear intervals repeated until their responses come readily and without strain. The shy child who may not yet be ready to sing an entire song is nevertheless often eager to participate. This is especially true when the question is personalized with his name or some object associated with him.

Call-and-response activity can be extended to include all the *pentatonic* tones and can be used to introduce new tones.

Rote learning with the descending minor third:

Suggested variations:

Who has a red shirt?
Who brought the cookies?
Who has a birthday?
Whose name is Jennifer?
Who went to Disneyland?
Who has brown shoes?

THERE WAS A MAN AND HE WAS MAD

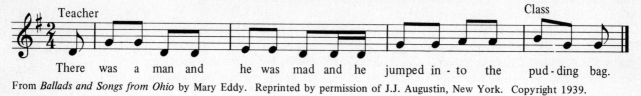

From *Ballads and Songs from Ohio* by Mary Eddy. Reprinted by permission of J.J. Augustin, New York. Copyright 1939.

DOWN CAME A LADY

Down came a la - dy, down came two, down came Miss Peg - gy Sue and she was dressed in blue.

From *Traditional Ballads of Virginia* by Arthur Kyle Davis. Reprinted by permission of the University Press of Virginia.

SALLY GO 'ROUND THE SUNSHINE

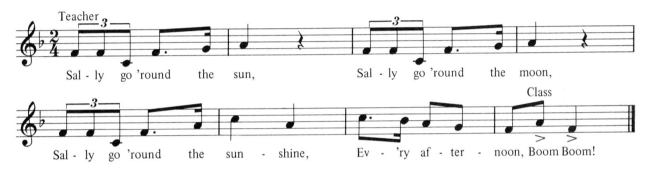

Sal - ly go 'round the sun, Sal - ly go 'round the moon,
Sal - ly go 'round the sun - shine, Ev - 'ry af - ter - noon, Boom Boom!

WHO'S THAT TAPPING AT THE WINDOW?

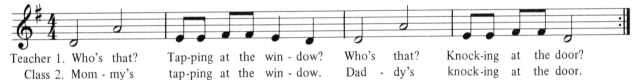

Teacher 1. Who's that? Tap-ping at the win - dow? Who's that? Knock-ing at the door?
Class 2. Mom - my's tap-ping at the win - dow. Dad - dy's knock-ing at the door.

"Who's That Tapping at the Window?" is from *American Folk Songs for Children* by Ruth Crawford Seeger.
Reprinted by permission of Curtis Brown, Ltd. Copyright, 1948, by Ruth Crawford Seeger.

LITTLE JACK HORNER

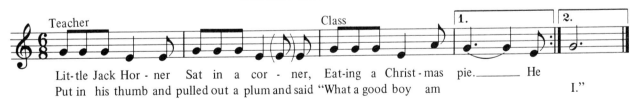

Lit-tle Jack Hor - ner Sat in a cor - ner, Eat-ing a Christ - mas pie._____ He
Put in his thumb and pulled out a plum and said "What a good boy am   I."

JACK BE NIMBLE

Jack be nim - ble, Jack be quick, And Juck jump o - ver the can - dle stick.

JOHNNY GET YOUR HAIR CUT

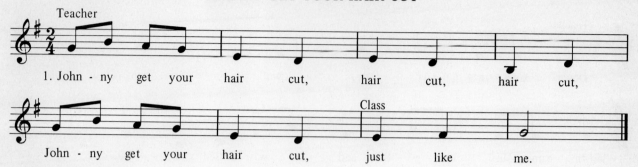

1. John - ny get your hair cut, hair cut, hair cut,
John - ny get your hair cut, just like me.

2. Sally has a new pen,
   New pen, new pen.
   Sally has a new pen,
   Just like me.

3. Jerry has a puppy,
   Puppy, puppy,
   Jerry has a puppy,
   Just like me.

From *Hill Country Tunes* by Samuel Preston Bayard. Reprinted by permission of American Folklore Society.

CREEP, MOUSE, CREEP

Angela Diller

Creep, Mouse, Creep! The old cat lies a - sleep; The
dog's a - way the Kit - tens play; Creep, Mouse, Creep.

From *PreSchool Music Book* by Angela Diller. Reprinted by permission of G. Schirmer, Inc. Copyright © 1936, 1964.
All rights reserved.

MARY WORE A RED DRESS

1. Ma - ry wore a red dress, _____ red dress, _____ red dress,
Ma - ry wore a red dress, _____ all day _____ long.

2. Jimmy wore a blue shirt,
   Blue shirt, blue shirt.
   Jimmy wore a blue shirt,
   All day long.

3. Cindy wore a pink dress,
   Pink dress, pink dress,
   Cindy wore a pink dress,
   All day long.

LITTLE TOM TINKER

THE PUMPKIN MAN

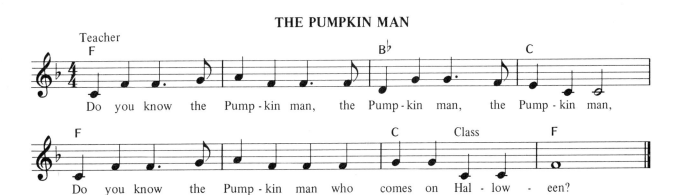

Choral Speaking and Chanting

Speech patterns derived from children's verses and games provide a rich source of introductory material for the beginning study of rhythm. In the primary curriculum the emphasis is on duple meter, with patterns comprised of the beat, its subdivision into half-beats, and the rest (silence) equal to the beat.

From the earliest lessons, children should be encouraged to listen to the teacher's changes in tempo and volume and to imitate these. As the children's responses to changes indicate increased perception, they should experiment with their own suggestions for tempo and volume changes.

The verses that follow are in duple meter, and for the convenience of later translation into rhythmic notation are written with the accented word at the beginning of each line.

Rhythm Notation   Verses in duple meter.

Phoebe rode a nanny goat.

Suzy broke her leg.

Father took his wedding coat and

Hung it on a peg.

One, two, three, four.

Mary at the cottage door.

Five, six, seven, eight.

Eating cherries off a plate.

Eena, deena, dina, duss.

Katla, weena, wina, wuss.

Spit, spot, must be done.

Twiddlum, twaddlum, twenty-one.

Ring-a-round the rosy. A

Pocket full of **posies**.

Hush, hush, hush, hush!   We

All fall down.

Bye, baby bun-ting.

Daddy's gone a-hun-ting to

Get a little rabbit skin to

Wrap his baby bunting in.

Wee Willie Winkie

Runs through the town.

Up-stairs and down-stairs

In his night gown.

Tapping at the window

Crying through the lock,

"Are the children in their beds?

Now it's eight o'clock."

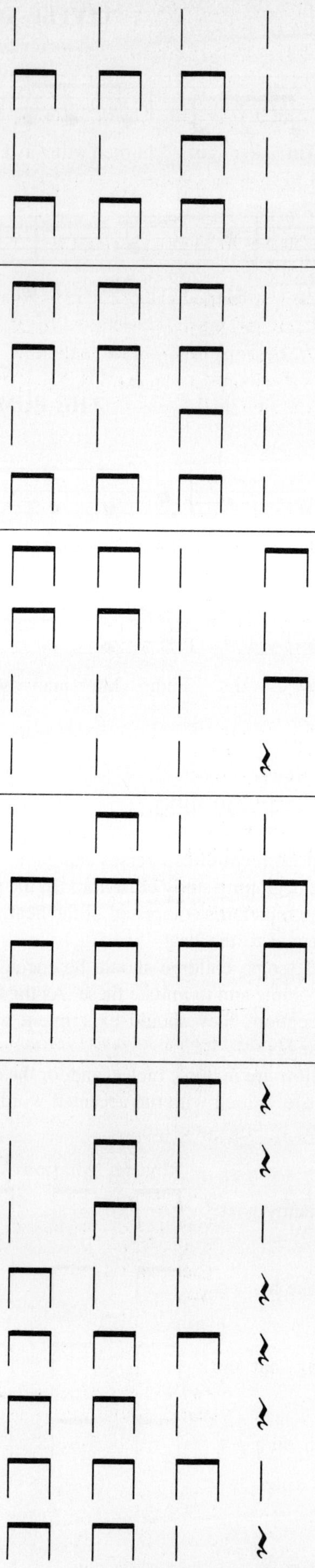

Peter Peter Pumpkin-Eater

Had a wife and couldn't keep her.

Put her in a pumpkin shell and

There she's doing very well.

The verses are always performed without monotony. Attention is given to the characteristics common to speech and musical inflection: *legato, staccato; accented* and *unaccented beats; crescendo, decrescendo; accelerando* and *ritardando* (see Glossary). The following children's verses suggest ways to teach beginning concepts. There are virtually unlimited possibilities for the creative use of speech patterns by the teacher and the students.

1. Dynamic changes

   pp Eena, deena, dina duss.
   f Katla, weena, wina, wuss.
   ff Spit, spot, must be done.
   pp Twiddlum, twaddlum, twenty-one.

2. Group with soloist

   Group Wee Willie Winkie
   Runs through the town,
   Upstairs and downstairs
   In his nightgown.

   Tapping at the window,
   Crying through the lock,

   Soloist "Are the children in their beds?
   Now it's eight o'clock."

3. Rhythmic ostinato

Have some of the class members tap the rhythm for the line, "Upstairs and downstairs," while the class chants the verse.

4. Instruments to accompany chanting

One two, three, four   X* X X X
Mary at the cottage door.   Mary at the cottage door.
Five, six, seven, eight.   X X XX X
Eating cherries off a   Eating cherries off a
plate   plate.

Ring-around the rosy. A
Pocket full of posies
Hush, hush, hush, hush! We
All fall *down.*   *cymbals and xylophone glissando are*
                                        played on the word "down"

*X = rhythm sticks

5. Canon

group 1:

Phoebe rode a nanny goat.
Suzy broke her leg.
Father took his wedding coat and
Hung it on a peg.

repeat

group 2:

silent first line
Phoebe rode a nanny goat.
Suzy broke her leg.
Father took his wedding coat and
Hung it on a peg.

repeat

From Speech to Melody

The verses presented in this section to be used as introductory material for children's first lessons may also be used to reinforce the beginning level intervals in teaching melody. The teacher should develop a repertoire of songs from the verses by assigning the descending minor third to the lyrics. For example:

The first songs

Hand signs indicating the range of the intervals are a good visual aid with beginning experiences in melody. For the first lessons the hand signs are used only with the words "higher lower." Later, when the children are matching tones correctly, the corresponding syllables of the *pentaton* are used. (sol-mi)

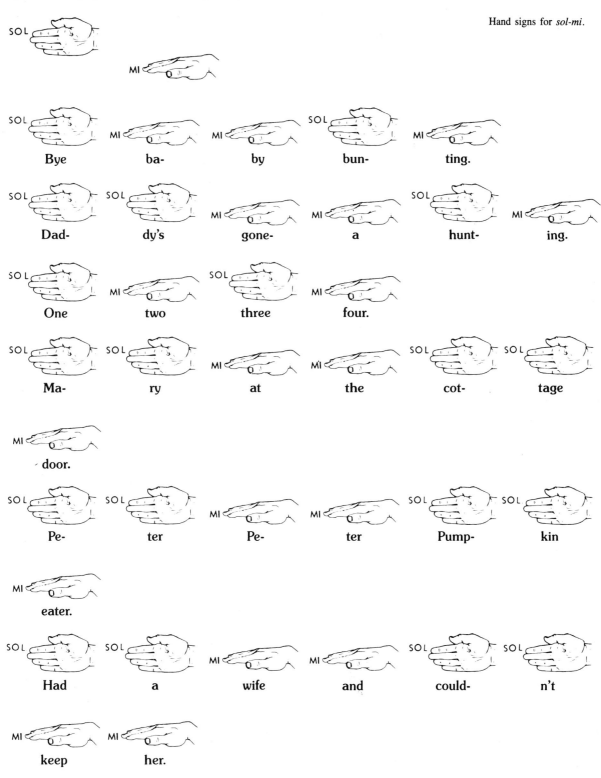

Hand signs for *sol-mi*.

SOL MI

SOL MI MI SOL MI
Bye ba- by bun- ting.

SOL SOL MI MI SOL MI
Dad- dy's gone- a hunt- ing.

SOL MI SOL MI
One two three four.

SOL SOL MI MI SOL SOL
Ma- ry at the cot- tage

MI
door.

SOL SOL MI MI SOL SOL
Pe- ter Pe- ter Pump- kin

MI
eater.

SOL SOL MI MI SOL SOL
Had a wife and could- n't

MI MI
keep her.

Pentatonic Scales and Songs

Teacher Preparation

Many of the songs and children's instrumental accompaniments for the primary years are built on the pentatonic scale, which includes five syllables in the sol-fa system. Corresponding numbers in the 8-note *diatonic* scale are 1, 2, 3, 5, and 6 (*do, re, mi, sol, la*).

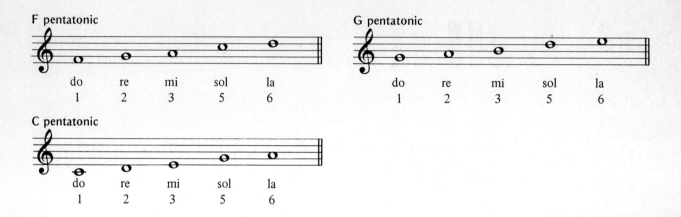

The complete scales look like this:

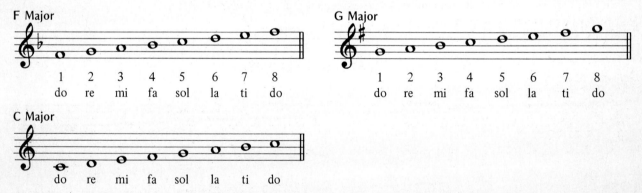

The flat ♭ and sharp ♯ may be omitted in materials for beginning readers, as the affected notes do not appear in pentatonic songs.

The syllables *fa* and *ti* are not introduced to children at this level because their presence requires the introduction of more advanced concepts like whole and half steps, the arrangement of whole and half steps in scales, and the relationships of scales and key signatures. These concepts are introduced later with the alphabetical names assigned to the staff lines and spaces. The teacher, however, will find them useful in locating accompaniment chords and in using the keyboard. Please note that *do* is movable, as are the numbers. The letter names are constant.

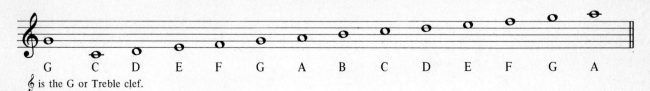

𝄞 is the G or Treble clef.

Locate the notes for the pentatonic scales on a keyboard.

F pentatonic

G pentatonic

C pentatonic

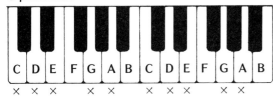

Following are some simple pentatonic songs with hand signs, durational syllables, and suggestions for accompaniments, movement, reading, and writing.

CLAP YOUR HANDS

Teaching Suggestions

1. Teach the rhythm patterns: | |, ⊓ |, ⊓ ⊓ using an echo-clapping exercise. Say "One, two, one, two," before starting to clap:

Echo clapping

	1	2	1	2
Teacher			⊓	
Students			⊓	

Teacher			
Students			
Teacher			
Students			

etc.

2. Do the echo exercise with stamping, clapping, and thigh slapping or patschen (left hand-left thigh; right hand-right thigh).

Teacher stamping

Students stamping

Teacher patschen

Students patschen

3. Teach the durational syllables for the rhythm patterns by rote. These are not written as words for children.

Durational syllables	say:	lyrics:
	ta ta	Clap clap
	ti-ti ta	Clap your hands
	ti-ti ti-ti	Clap your hands to-
	ta ta	geth-er.

4. Vary the dynamics by suggestions through new lyrics.

Teacher:	Clap, clap, clap your hands.
	Clap your hands so *softly*.
Children:	
(clapping softly)	X X XX X
	XX XX X X
Teacher:	Clap clap clap your hands.
	Clap your hands so *loudly*.

5.   Divide the class into two groups. Use a question-and-answer format in a movement exercise.

Group I (clapping):	X X XX X
Group II (stamping):	XX XX X X
Group I (tapping):	X X XX X
Group II (patschen):	XX XX X X

6. Review the hand signs for *sol* and *mi*.

sol   mi   sol-sol mi
sol-sol mi-mi sol   mi

7. Reading rhythm and melody: Use the stem notation to indicate the rhythm. The melodic syllables may be shown with the rhythm in this way:

2 beats

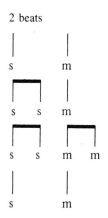

The placement of the notes on the staff is shown in an enlarged format. *Do* is found at this sign: ╞

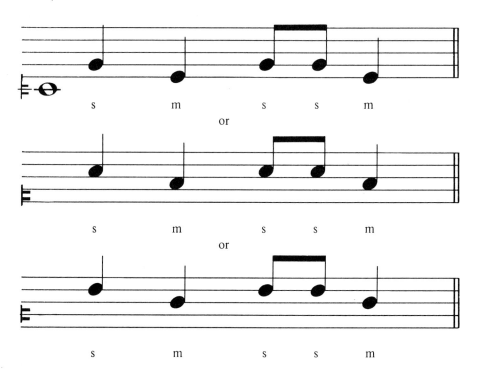

Sol and *mi* on the staff

RAIN, RAIN, GO AWAY

In teaching songs to preschool and elementary age children, teachers should be aware of the comfortable vocal ranges suitable for the earliest songs, and an expanded range which is developed in the upper elementary grades.

Youngest voices   Primary years   Intermediate and upper years

For each song, the teacher must give the starting pitch and indicate the tempo. The pitch must be accurate, and the teacher should use a pitch pipe, resonator bell, or piano to locate the starting note.

Teacher Preparation

On your piano locate the pitches used in "Rain, Rain."

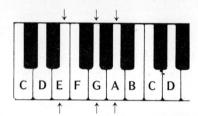

The song may be accompanied by one chord on your autoharp or guitar. Locate the C Major bar on the autoharp. Strum the chord on the first beat of each measure. The hand position for this chord on the guitar is shown below.

A one-chord accompaniment

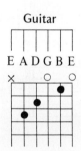

On your guitar, practice the folk strum known as the "brush strum." This is a downward motion with the thumb across the strings.

READING AND WRITING PRACTICE: Three Pentatonic Scales

Write the C, F, and G pentatonic scales (*do, re, mi, sol, la*).

The placement of *do* on the staves below is indicated by the sign ⊨. Write the notes named beneath each staff, then create an exercise for children using la, sol, and mi.

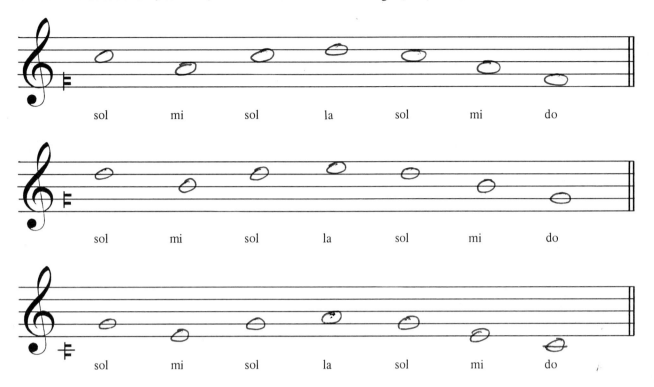

sol   mi   sol   la   sol   mi   do

sol   mi   sol   la   sol   mi   do

sol   mi   sol   la   sol   mi   do

Locate each *do* on the piano. Sing each exercise. Create new exercises using the same syllables and play or sing them for your class to write.

LUCY LOCKET

La Sol Mi

Lu - cy Lock - et   lost her pock - et,   Kit - ty Fish - er   found   it,

Not   a   pen - ny   was there   in   it,   on - ly   rib - bon   round   it.

Teacher Preparation

Plan to sing the song to the children or your methods class in its entirety first. Then break the song into sections for the class to imitate in rote style.

Teacher:	Lucy Locket lost her pocket
Children:	*Repeat*
Teacher:	Kitty Fisher found it
Children:	*Repeat*
Teacher:	*Both lines above with children repeating*

> Teacher: Not a penny was there in it
> Children: *Repeat*
> Teacher: Only ribbon 'round it
> Children: *Repeat*

Repeat the second half of the song as above. Then have the class sing the whole song with you.

Teaching Suggestion

Use the song to introduce the Curwen hand sign for the sol-fa syllable *la*. Ask the class to follow your hand signs as they sing the syllables and the lyrics.

Hand sign for *la*

Then have the class use hand signs as they sing.

LITTLE SALLY WATER

La Sol Mi

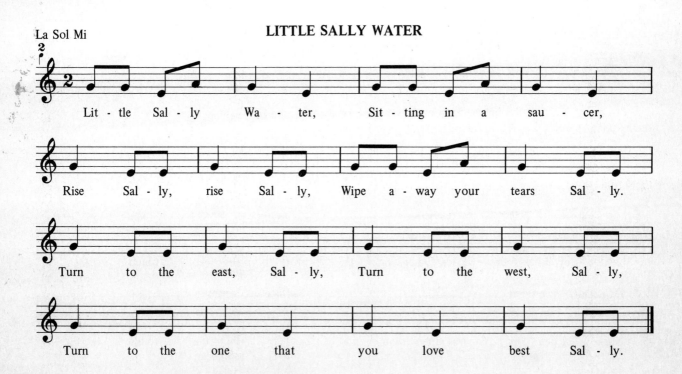

Teaching Suggestions

1. Use this accompaniment for children to play simultaneously on Orff instruments.

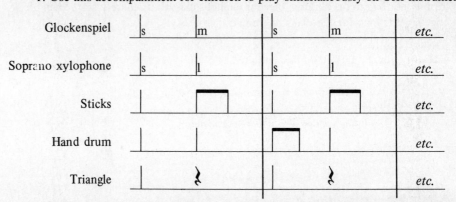

2. Movement Game: Have children step in a circle on the beat. One child sits in the center while acting out the lyrics. At the end of the song he or she chooses a successor and the game continues. The child's name may be used in place of "Sally Water."

3. Prepare the students to perform their own accompaniment and to read the rhythmic notation of the song with this echo-clapping exercise. Count aloud before beginning to clap:

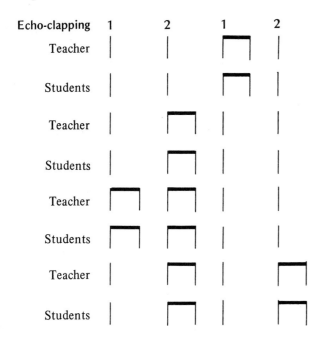

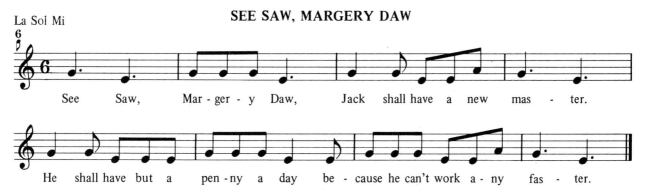

Teacher Preparation

Meter is the grouping of beats into twos, threes, fours, sixes, etc. and is shown at the beginning of a musical work by a meter signature, or time signature. The upper numeral indicates the number of beats to be performed in each group; the lower numeral indicates which note is to receive one beat.

Meters, time signatures, note values

A time signature of $\frac{6}{8}$ as in "See Saw," tells us that there will be six beats per measure and that the eighth note will receive one beat. (Sometimes the lower numeral is replaced by the note itself, as in $\frac{6}{\flat}$ or $\frac{3}{\flat}$. This system helps to clarify the full meaning of the time signature for beginning readers.)

Each grouping of beats makes up a measure. Measures are separated by bar lines. A double bar denotes the end of a song or instrumental piece.

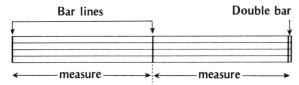

Learn the note values for the common meters in elementary music.

Time signatures: **♩** or **2/4** ; **♩** or **3/4** ; **♩** or **4/4**

Note values (beats per note): ♩ = 1 ♩ = 2 ♩. = 3 𝅝 = 4

♪ = $\frac{1}{2}$

♪ = $\frac{1}{4}$

Time signature: **♩** or **6/8**

Note value (beats per note): ♪ = $\frac{1}{2}$ ♪ = 1 ♩ = 2 ♩. = 3 ♩ = 4 ♩. = 6

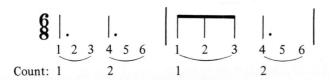

Count: 1   2   1   2

Teaching Suggestions

1. To reinforce the hand sign for *la*, practice "See Saw" using the signs for *sol*, *mi*, and *la*. Note that the new syllable appears first on the word "new." (*Note:* Rhythmic notation is not shown. Melodic contour is shown with hand signs.)

2. Have children sway left and then right on the accented syllables.

Sway Left: See saw
      Right: Margery Daw
       Left: Jack shall have a new
       etc.   Master.
            He shall have but a
            Penny a day. Be-
            cause he can't work any
            Faster.

3. In preparation for a simple autoharp accompaniment, strum (away from the body) on each of the accented syllables above. Have each child strum the autoharp while the teacher or another child presses the C Major bar.

BELL HORSES

La Sol Mi

Bell   hor - ses,   Bell   hor - ses,   What's   the   time   o'   day?

One   o' - clock,   Two   o' - clock,   Time   to   a - way.

Teaching Suggestions

1. The song "Bell Horses" can be used to introduce the "extended ta" in rhythm.

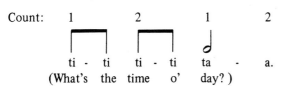

Count: 1   2   1   2

ti - ti   ti - ti   ta   -   a.
(What's   the   time   o'   day?)

To teach this new concept, write this pattern for the children and have them recite it.

1   2   1   2   The half note

ti - ti   ti - ti   ta   ta

Now connect the two ta's.

ti - ti   ti - ti   ta_____a

Tell the students that you will make only one beginning sound for the two ta's.
The new note looks like this: 𝅗𝅥

Write the rhythm of the new song.

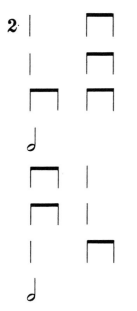

Ask the students to tap the rhythm along with you as you read the stem notation.

2. Have the students sing the melodic syllables with hand signs.

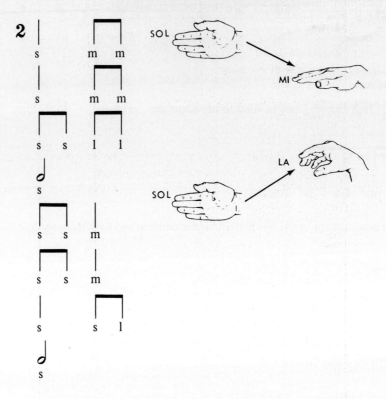

3. Prepare the students to perform their own accompaniment by having them:

Clap the rhythm of the song.
Clap, tap, or step the basic beats of the song while singing.
Practice mallet motions in the air on the beats of the song.

1 2	Mallets or Stepping	
Béll hórses	Left	Right
Béll hórses	Left	Right
Whát's the tíme o'	Left	Right
Dáy?	Left	Right
Óne o'clóck	Left	Right
Twó o'clóck	Left	Right
Tíme tó a	Left	Right
Wáy.	Left	Right

4. Have children accompany "Bell Horses" with Orff instruments using this scheme:

Woodblocks								
Soprano xylophone	s	l	s	l	s	l	s	l
Alto xylophone	m		m		m		m	
Sleigh bells								

5. Work with the children's suggestions for creation of an "arrangement" of "Bell Horses" that demonstrates the various concepts they've learned.

Creating an arrangement

Introduction: woodblocks
First time through: singing words
Second time through: singing with instruments
Third time through: saying durational syllables
Fourth time through: stepping to the beat while singing
Coda: woodblocks and instruments

Other possibilities include varying dynamics, small group-large group contrasts, singing sol-fa syllables, and combining the song with another pentatonic song.

6. Use doweling, popsicle sticks, or felt pieces, with some cut to the size of the stem and some cut to the size of the beam.

Stem   Beam

Each child should have a supply of these to arrange on his desk for dictation. The teacher may use a drum or clap the rhythm, which the student then "writes" with the sticks or cloth. The beginning exercises should be brief and review only those patterns which the children have sung in their songs and clapped in their echo games.

Rhythmic dictation

Teacher says   one,   two
                    one,   two

Claps

IT'S RAINING

La Sol Mi

It's rain - ing, it's pour - ing, the old man is snor - ing,

Went to bed and he bumped his head and he did-n't get up in the morn - ing.

Teacher Preparation

1. Say the durational syllables that correspond to the note values of this song in $\frac{4}{4}$. Note that the first measure is incomplete (only one beat). This unaccented beat on "it's" is called an *upbeat,* or *anacrusis.* It is considered to be beat four of the last measure. When counting the anacrusis, organize the beats this way:

Upbeat

The upbeat

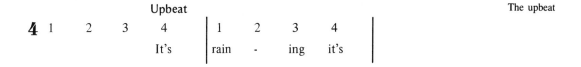

2. Practice using the hand signs for la, sol, and mi to show the contour of the melody as your class sings the syllables.

3. Find the three notes of this song on a piano. Play the starting pitch for your class before they sing through the lyrics with you.

HOT CROSS BUNS

Mi Re Do

Hot cross buns.   Hot cross buns.   One - a - pen -ny, two - a - pen-ny,   hot cross buns.

HOP OLD SQUIRREL

Mi Re Do

Hop old Squirrel*,   ei - dle-dum, ei - dle-dum,   Hop old squirrel,   ei - dle -dum dee;

Hop old squirrel,   ei - dle - dum, ei - dle - dum,   Hop old squirrel,   ei - dle - dum dee!

Reprinted by permission of the publishers from *On the Trail of Negro Folk Songs*, by Dorothy Scarborough. Cambridge, Mass.: Harvard University Press, Copyright 1925 by Harvard University Press, Copyright 1953 by Mary McDaniel Parker.

* Squirrel is pronounced as one syllable.

Teacher Preparation

"Hot Cross Buns" and "Hop Old Squirrel" can be accompanied on the autoharp or guitar by the F Major chord, which is strummed on the first and third beats of each measure.

Hót cross búns

Hót cross búns

Oné-a-penny, twó-a-penny,

Hót cross búns.

Locate the notes for these songs on the piano keyboard.

Teaching Suggestions

1. Children may participate in the autoharp accompaniment by strumming or holding down the chord bar. Have them practice strumming "in the air" first, away from their bodies on the accented beats.

2. Use these two songs to introduce *re* and the appropriate hand sign

Re and its hand sign

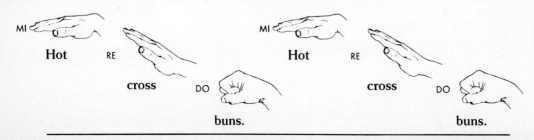

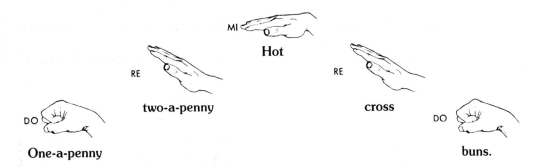

3. Introduce the rest 𝄽 , or silence, with the song "Hot Cross Buns." The durational syllable is "shh."

(Some teachers prefer to have children make a motion with their arms to signify the rest. The "shh" sound may be more difficult to control.)

Beats	1	2	3	4		The rest
Hot Cross Buns	ta	ta	ta	shh		
Hot Cross Buns	ta	ta	ta	shh		
One-a-penny, two-a-penny	ti-ti	ti-ti	ti-ti	ti-ti		
Hot Cross Buns	ta	ta	ta	ta		

4 or $\frac{4}{}$ in place of the conventional time signature; indicates that there are four ta's or quarter notes per measure.

4. Explain that ⊨ is used to indicate the placement of *do* in a song.

5. Rhythm instrument accompaniment for "Hop Old Squirrel":

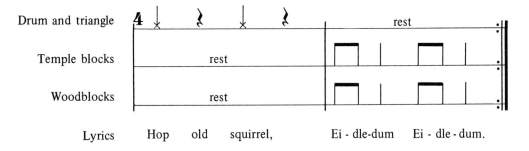

| | Lyrics | Hop | old | squirrel, | Ei - dle-dum | Ei - dle - dum. |

6. Lead the students in the following movement activity: children move in a circle, or a line, hopping forward on the words "hop" and "squirrel." They stand in place and patschen on the words "eidledum, eidledum." Ask the children to find like and different places in the rhythm of the songs. Use geometric forms beside the lines of rhythmic notation to show the form of the songs.

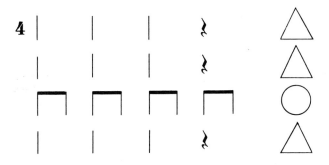

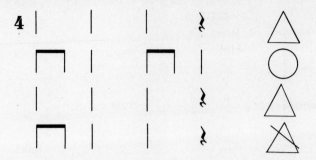

7. Ask the class to experiment with dynamic contrasts by singing "eidledum, eidledum" softly. Then have them sing "Hop old squirrel" more softly than "eidledum."

A Verse in $\frac{4}{4}$ for Chanting, Moving, and Playing

	Rhythmic Notation	Movement
Sing a song of sixpence a	**4** ⊓ ⊓ |	⊓	patschen
Pocket full of rye;	⊓ ⊓ | 𝄾	clap
Four and twenty blackbirds,	⊓ ⊓ | |	snap
Baked in a pie.	| ⊓ | 𝄾	stamp
When the pie was opened the	⊓ ⊓ | ⊓	patschen
Birds began to sing.	⊓ ⊓ | 𝄾	clap
Wasn't that a dainty dish to	⊓ ⊓ ⊓ ⊓	tap head
Set before the King?	⊓ ⊓ | 𝄾	clap

Teaching Suggestions

1. Try this verse as a chant with dynamics. Experiment with *crescendo* and *decrescendo*. Try the entire verse ⟨ and ⟩. Try accenting key words in the verse, or stretching out a line like a musical *rubato*.

Wasn't   THAT   a dain-ty dish to...

2. Use the verse as the basis for a rhythm band piece. In the following suggested version there is a question and answer format, with woodblocks always assigned to the same pattern.

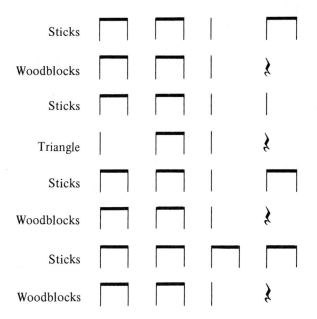

WRITING AND SINGING PRACTICE: Mi Re Do

1. Write the notes that are named beneath each staff. The sign ╞ shows you the location of *do*.

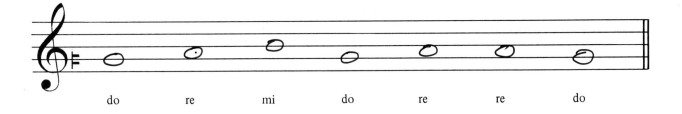

do re mi do re re do

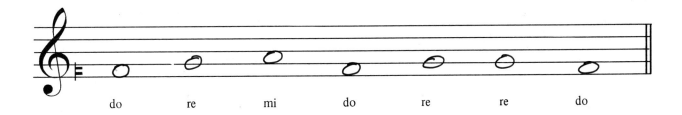

do re mi do re re do

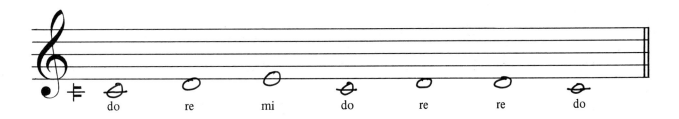

do re mi do re re do

2. Sing the exercises shown above. Remember to locate each *do* on the piano or pitch pipe. Now sing each pattern using scale numbers and letter names of the notes.

GOOD NEWS!

Teaching Suggestions

1. Teach the anacrusis, or upbeat, through this lively spiritual. Ask the children to patschen or stamp on "news" each time they sing it. This activity helps them place the stress on the first beat of the first complete measure. (The song should be learned by rote: the anacrusis is not presented formally with notation until the children have learned several songs which present this concept.)

2. Use an autoharp accompaniment:

Notate the accompaniment for the class with stem notation. Young children make the chord changes very easily if they are color-coded. (G Major chord: blue; D7 chord: red.)

3. Have the class try variations in singing the song:

    a. Xylophones, tone bars, or glockenspiel play on the words "Good news!"

Variations on a song

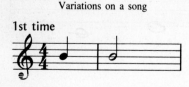
1st time

2nd time

3rd time

b. Two groups: Each group sings part of the phrase:

Group I:	Good news!
Group II:	Chariot's comin'.
Group I:	Good news!
Group II:	Chariot's comin'.
Group I:	Good news!
Group II:	Chariot's comin'.
All:	And I don't want it to leave me behind.

    c. Perform the above twice. Sing the second time very softly. Show the class that the sign indicating soft voices is *p* and the sign indicating loud voices is *f*.

    d. Use resonator bells to accompany:

For G Major chord find bars G, B, D.
For D₇ chord find bars D, F♯, A, C.

Distribute the seven bars with mallets. Ask the children to follow the accompaniment chart for the autoharp.

LISTENING AND WRITING PRACTICE: Mi Re Do

1. The first note in each exercise is notated for you. Listen to its pitch as it is played for you. Then notate the remaining pitches as they are played or sung for you.

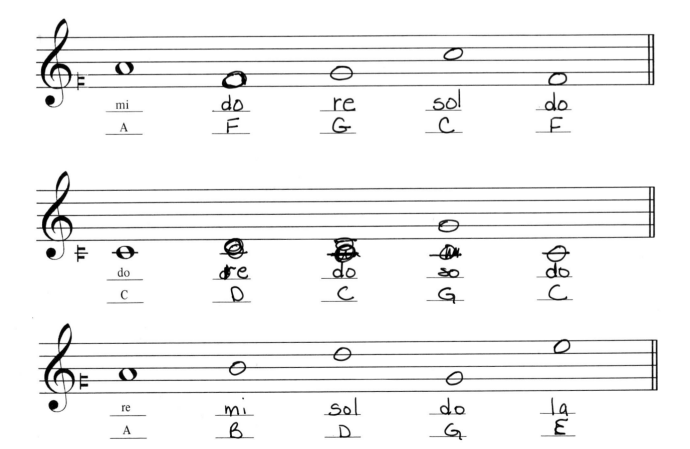

2. Using the syllables *mi, re,* and *do,* make up your own exercise with the rhythm indicated below. Then sing it, play it on the piano, and practice the hand signs.

Sol Mi Re Do

THAT'S A MIGHTY PRETTY MOTION

That's a might-y pret-ty mo-tion, Dee, di, dee, That's a might-y pret-ty mo-tion, Dee, di, dee, That's a might-y pret-ty mo-tion, Dee, di, dee, Rise, Su-gar, rise!

Teacher Preparation

Learn this song by rote, and practice teaching it to your class. Sing the entire song. Then give them one phrase at a time. Remember to give the singers the beginning pitch. In this case you should give B, A, and G (*mi, re, do*) the three opening pitches, since the song begins on *mi* rather than *do.*

Teaching Suggestions

1. Ask the class to form a circle and select one person to be in the middle. The children in the circle perform movements while singing by bending their knees on beats one and three, and clapping on beats 2 and 4.

Movement activity in a stationary circle

The child in the center steps or claps to the rhythm of the song. On "Rise, Sugar, Rise!" that child selects a new child to act out the rhythm and joins the circle.

2. Ask the class to listen for places in the melody and rhythm that are identical, and a section that is different. Use paper for cardboard cutouts to illustrate the song's form.

That's a mighty pretty motion, dee-di-dee, ◯

That's a mighty pretty motion, dee-di-dee. ◯

That's a mighty pretty motion, dee-di-dee, ◯

Rise, sugar, rise. △

Sol Mi Re Do

MARY HAD A LITTLE LAMB

Ma - ry had a lit - tle lamb, lit - tle lamb, lit - tle lamb,
Ev' - ry - where that Ma - ry went, Ma - ry went, Ma - ry went.

Ma - ry had a lit - tle lamb, its fleece was white as snow. And
Ev' - ry - where that Ma - ry went the lamb was sure to go.

Sol Mi Re Do

LET US CHASE THE SQUIRREL

Let us chase the squir - rel, Up the hick - 'ry, down the hick - 'ry,

Let us chase the squir - rel, Up the hick - 'ry tree.

Teacher Preparation

To use an autoharp accompaniment, prepare a classroom chart for children using colors to indicate the chord changes, such as blue for G Major and red for D_7.

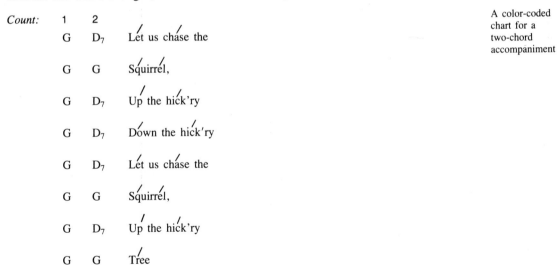

A color-coded
chart for a
two-chord
accompaniment

Count:	1	2	
	G	D_7	Let us chase the
	G	G	Squirrel,
	G	D_7	Up the hick'ry
	G	D_7	Down the hick'ry
	G	D_7	Let us chase the
	G	G	Squirrel,
	G	D_7	Up the hick'ry
	G	G	Tree

Teaching Suggestions

1. Ask the class to sing the song several times, making the tempo faster and faster. Have them try to sing more softly as the tempo increases.

2. Have a child play the xylophone on a *glissando,* sliding the mallet from G–G with an up motion and a down motion on "up the hick'ry, down the hick'ry."

3. Divide the group into two sections and try the song in *canon* style, with one group beginning after the other has completed a measure and following in strict imitation to the end of the song.

BOUGHT ME A CAT

Sol Mi Re Do

1. Bought me a cat and the cat pleased me,

Fed my cat un - der yon - der tree.

Cat went Fid - dle - i - fee, Fid - dle - i - fee.

2. Bought me a hen and the hen pleased me,
3. Bought me a duck and the duck pleased me,

Fed my hen un - der yon - der tree.
Fed my duck un - der yon - der tree.

Repeat verse 3 only

2+3. Hen went Chip - sy, Chop - sy, Cat went
3. Duck went slish - y, slosh - y,

fid - dle - i - fee, Fid - dle - i - fee.

Teaching Suggestions

1. Review the melodic syllable *re* by rote.
2. Let the children sing "fiddle-i-fee, fiddle-i-fee" by themselves. Show the contour of the response with the hand signs.

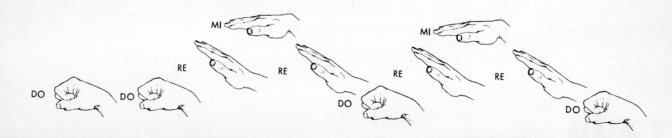

3. Autoharp accompaniment for the teacher:

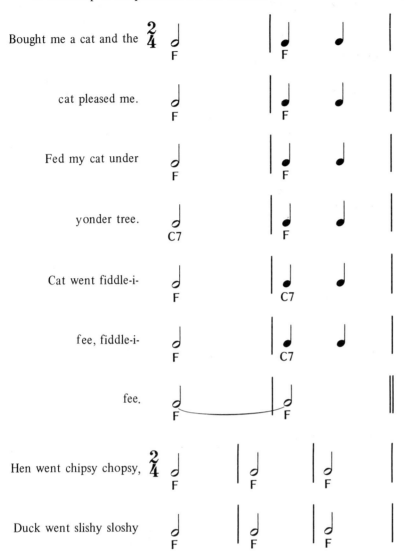

WHO'S THAT TAPPING AT THE WINDOW?

Sol Mi Re Do

Who's that? Tap-ping at the win-dow. Who's that? Knock-ing at the door.

Mom-my's tap-ping at the win-dow. Dad-dy's knock-ing at the door.

Teaching Suggestions

1. Teach the ascending interval *do-sol* with this song. Practice the hand signals:

The ascending interval *do-sol*

Who's that?
Mommy's
Daddy's

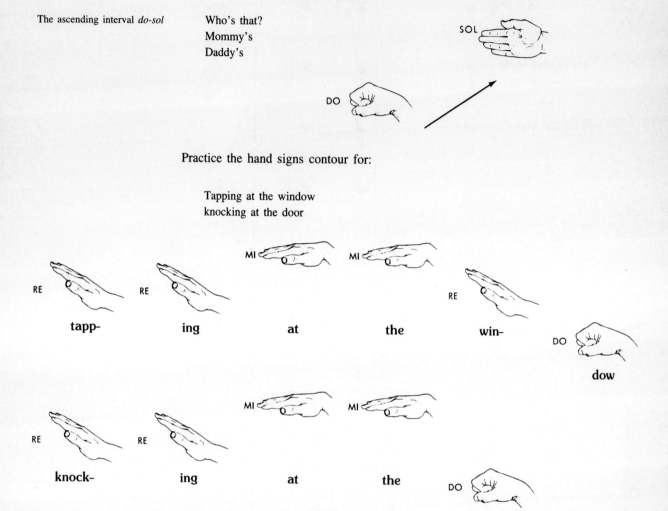

Practice the hand signs contour for:

Tapping at the window
knocking at the door

2. To review the extended ta (ta-a) durational syllable, have the children sway and tap as they sing the song:

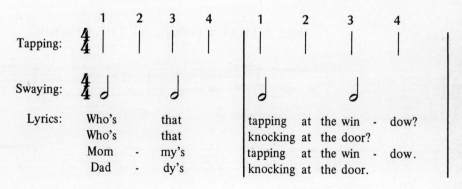

	1	2	3	4	1	2	3	4

Tapping:

Swaying:

Lyrics:

Who's	that		tapping	at	the	win	-	dow?
Who's	that		knocking	at	the	door?		
Mom	-	my's	tapping	at	the	win	-	dow.
Dad	-	dy's	knocking	at	the	door.		

Write the notation sequence, proceeding from the known ta pattern.

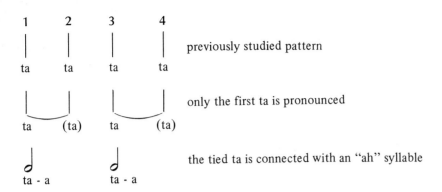

3. Use Orff xylophone or tone bar instrumental accompaniment, alternating with a rhythm instrument:

Instruments   **Notation and Lyrics**

4. Review the rhythm patterns using this echo clapping exercise:

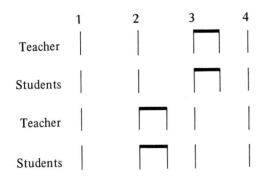

Teacher

Students

Teacher

Students

* Hands together and motion outward to indicate continued sound of half note.

  5. Write these rhythm patterns on cards or tags that can be folded into a child's hand. The patterns are derived from the beginning folk song repertoire.

Review of quarter and eighth notes and quarter rests

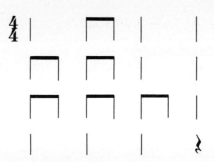

  Ask the children to walk in a circle. Establish the beat for walking using a hand drum or woodblocks. Then play the patterns given to the children. Perform them, repeating each one. When a child recognizes her pattern, she steps into the circle and steps to the rhythm of her pattern until she hears a different one. Then another child steps into the circle to step the new pattern, and so on.

  6. Have the class find sections of the melody that are repeated. Assist them in indicating the form of the song with geometric figures.

A lesson in form

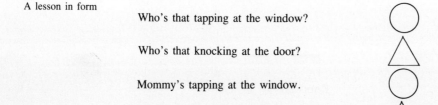

Who's that tapping at the window?

Who's that knocking at the door?

Mommy's tapping at the window.

Daddy's knocking at the door.

DINAH

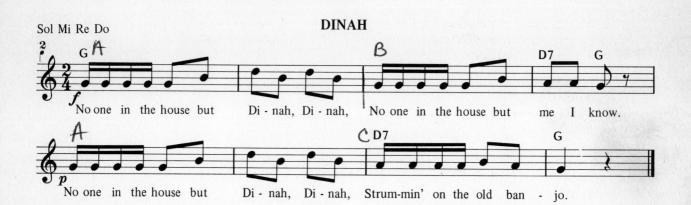

Sol Mi Re Do

No one in the house but Di - nah, Di - nah, No one in the house but me I know.

No one in the house but Di - nah, Di - nah, Strum-min' on the old ban - jo.

Teacher Preparation

1. Practice the hand signs for *do-mi-sol-mi-do,* working with a partner and then with your methods class to be sure that your signals are showing the relationships of the pitches.

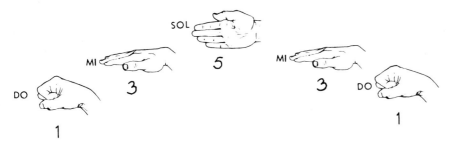

2. Prepare and practice from a two-chord accompaniment chart, using blue to represent G Major and red for D_7.

Guitar: Use the sweep strum (downward motion with thumb on all strings) for the ta's, or quarter notes. Practice a brush strum, using the backs of the first and second fingers, on the ti-ti's, or divided beats.

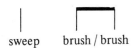

sweep   brush / brush

Autoharp: Use a full sweep on the ta's and small strokes in the middle range of the strings for the ti-ti's.

Teaching Suggestions

1. Introduce the sixteenth note pattern 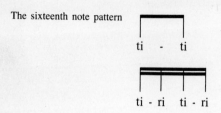, which is the equivalent of one beat (ta, or quarter note) in this song. Tell the class that you are dividing each part of the ti-ti into two notes.

The sixteenth note pattern

Say the durational syllables:

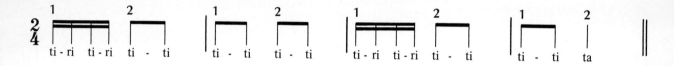

2. Ask the children to sing very softly (*pp*, or *pianissimo*) on the second half of the song. Have the class experiment with dynamic changes of their choice.

3. *Movement activity:* Ask the class to walk the rhythm that you play on a drum. Start with the basic four beat pattern and then change to patterns using subdivided beats. Ask the class to express changes in dynamics with large heavy motions for loud patterns, and small, light motions for soft patterns.

GRANDMA GRUNTS

Teacher Preparation

Prepare an autoharp or guitar accompaniment:

Autoharp: Use long, full sweeps over all the strings on half notes, and short strokes in the middle range of the strings for the quarter notes.

Teaching Suggestions

1. Use resonator bells to highlight the ascending fifth interval:

Play on:
"curious thing"
"heard her say"
(whistle)

do do sol
1 1 5

Also try the bells on the descending intervals:

Play on:
"girls must sing"
"yesterday"
"la-la-la"

mi re do
3 2 1

2. Divide the class into two sections or group/soloist to perform the song in a call-and-response style.

> I: Grandma Grunts said a curious thing,
> II: "Boys can whistle, but girls must sing."
> I: This is what I heard her say,
> II: Twas no longer than yesterday,
> I: Boys can whistle
> II: (whistle)
> All: Girls can sing, tra-la-la-la-la.

WRITING PRACTICE: Syllables, Letter Names of Notes, and Rhythmic Dictation

Write the melodic syllables, letter names of the notes, and scale numbers of the notes shown below. Play each exercise on the piano and practice singing with the hand signs. Write a similar lesson for a children's group.

Notate the rhythm notation that is performed for you. The first measure is shown.

RING AROUND THE ROSY

Teaching Suggestion

Children should develop their ability to "hear" a song while in a silent environment, and to maintain a steady pulse as they think through the melody. Ask the children to sing the first two measures of "Ring Around the Rosy" and then remain silent until the last measure when they all sing "down." For the first few lessons in which you use this activity it is a good idea to have the class walk on the beats while they are thinking the tune.

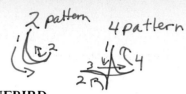

[handwritten: 2 pattern   4 pattern]

[handwritten top margin: 2 pattern   4 pattern]

[handwritten: Marcato]

La Sol Mi Re Do

HERE COMES A BLUEBIRD

Here comes a blue - bird through the ___ win - dow,
Hey, did - dle dum a day day day. Take a lit - tle part - ner,
hop in the gar - den, Hey, did - dle dum a day day day.

Teaching Suggestions

[handwritten: Tue. Apr. 10 – Select rythmic pattern for accompainament denote color for each chord change at the top (legend) chart on paper – work bells into Bluebird –]

1. Help the students see similarities and differences in form by preparing a chart or chalkboard to display 2-measure groups from this song (read left to right).

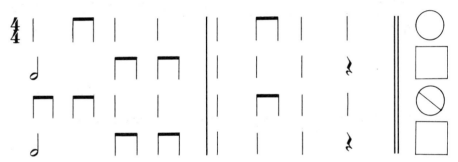

Prepare adhesive symbols to indicate like and unlike groups. Ask the class if line 2 is the same as or different from line 1; if 3 is the same as 2, etc. Finally, is line 3 *exactly* like line 1?

[handwritten: = Groups work on auto harp –]

2. *Movement activity:* The children form a circle and join hands, lifting their arms to form arches. One child is "bluebird," and goes in and out of the circle through the "windows." He takes a partner as indicated and they hop around the circle. The partner becomes "bluebird," the first child joins the ring, and the song is repeated. The song can be varied for sustained interest with different instrumental accompaniments, melodic syllables, and humming on the repeated sections.

[handwritten: Legato]

[handwritten right margin: 3 pattern]

La Sol Mi Re Do

COFFEE GROWS ON WHITE OAK TREES

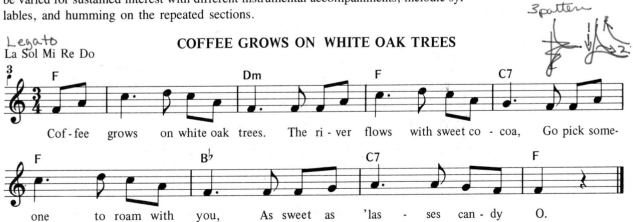

Cof - fee grows on white oak trees. The ri - ver flows with sweet co - coa, Go pick some-
one to roam with you, As sweet as 'las - ses can - dy O.

Teacher Preparation

Practice this autoharp or guitar accompaniment, stressing the first beat of each measure.

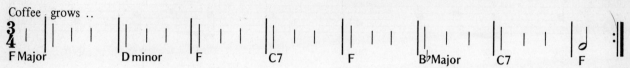

Teaching Suggestions

1. Use the song as one of the rote introductions to the dotted quarter.

2. *Circle Dance:* Have the class form a circle of partners who face one another. Try this sequence:

A circle dance in triple meter

First time through: group sings verse and moves on a stamp/clap/clap pattern, emphasizing the accented beats.

Second time through: group sings the song on ''la.'' Partners join hands and step counterclockwise, bending their knees slightly on the accented beats, first the right foot, then the left.

Rlr   lrl   rlr   lrl   etc.

Third time through: group hums. Partners face one another and sway in opposite directions on the accented beats.

Teacher Preparation

1. Write out the melodic syllables below this rhythmic notation.

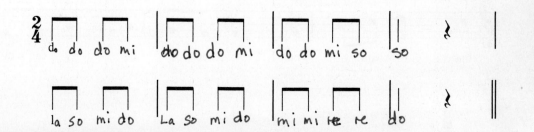

2. Practice this autoharp accompaniment, which includes only two chords.

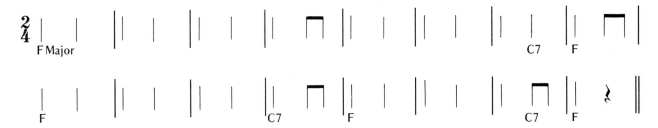

3. Practice singing the song while stepping to the beat and clapping the rhythm of the lyrics. Then step the rhythm of the lyrics while clapping the beats.

Teaching Suggestion

Ask the class to compare the phrases of this song to one another. What is the melodic contour of the first 4 measures? The second group of 4 measures? Are there any repeated phrases?

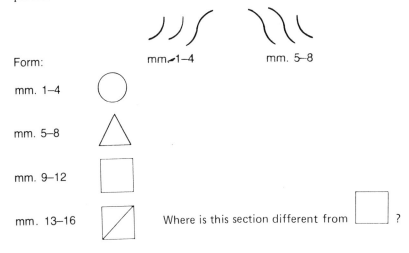

BUTTON YOU MUST WANDER

Teaching Suggestions

1. This is a good song for reinforcing reading skills. Write this notation on the board:

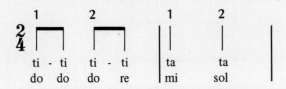

Ask the children how many times they hear this pattern in the song.
2. Review the syllables and hand signs.

Review of *la sol mi re do*

do do do re mi sol
re sol mi do
do do do re mi sol
re sol do.

la la la sol mi
la la la sol mi.

do do do re mi sol
re sol do.

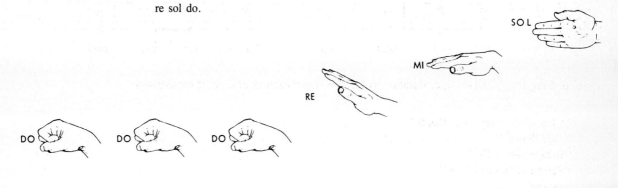

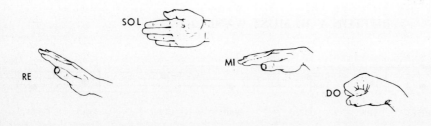

3. Have everyone sit in a circle and sway to the accented beats.

     L   R
Button you must wander

     L   R
Wander Wander

     L   R
Button you must wander

    L   R
Ev'ry where.

       etc.

A button is passed around the circle. A child sitting in the center tries to guess who has the
button when the music stops. If she guesses correctly, the button-keeper becomes "it"
and takes his place in the center.

4. Student's instrumental part for xylophone or song bell with letter names of notes:

5. Sing syllables (sol-fa or durational) for first two measures of each of these songs.

"Clap, Clap, Clap Your Hands"
"Bell Horses"
"Bought Me A Cat"
"See Saw, Margery Daw"
"Button"

Ask students which song they hear.

Part 3

Songs with the Extended Pentaton: Intermediate Concepts in Rhythm and Movement

When children have learned to sing pentatonic songs in a comfortable range, have developed their reading and writing skills to include C, F, and G pentatonic tones, and can perform imitative movement and simple improvisations, they are ready for more challenging work. The grade level does not determine the content of the curriculum; the children's readiness does. "Intermediate" refers to grades three and four if the students have received appropriate instruction in grades K–2.

At this level the study of the extended pentaton brings a wealth of song material to the class. Rhythmic awareness is enhanced by work with triple and compound meter songs and pieces, syncopation, and moving circle and parallel line dances. Accompaniments are developed for bells, autoharps, and guitars to prepare the ear for the study of harmonic concepts in the upper grades. Body movements are performed as accompaniments too, and two-part singing is continued with echo songs. The playing of the Orff instruments is carefully prepared with "mirror" movements. There is increased attention to form in the songs, as children find like and different phrases in the scores. Children at this level can identify a song by hearing its rhythm or melody or by seeing its score. Melodic improvisation on the rhythms of verses becomes an important part of the creative process.

The children's suggestions for ways in which to perform the songs, play the instruments, and move to the music are vital to their development. They need to experience in their formative years the feelings and pride associated with creating something that is their own.

CHARLIE OVER THE OCEAN

Teacher Preparation

1. Practice the hand signs for *do-sol₁*, an interval that is a descending fourth. The interval appears at the beginning of the well-known song, "Old MacDonald". Note that the *sol* below *do* is indicated with a special mark: *sol₁*.

The descending interval, *do-sol₁*

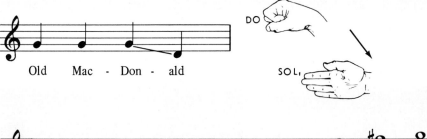

2. Children need to practice the motions they will use with mallet instruments before they play ostinato patterns. Teacher preparation for this activity should include lessons in which the methods class "mirrors" the motions of the teacher. These motions, of course, are the reverse of the motions indicated on the printed score: right-left-right-left becomes left-right-left-right. Here are the motions to practice before a group to prepare for the instrumental accompaniment.

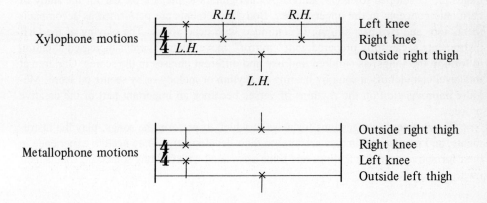

Teaching Suggestion

Divide the class into two sections. These may be of equal size, a large group and a small group, a group and soloist(s), or vocal and instrumental groups. Each line of the song is repeated by Group II or the soloist or the instrumental section. If the response group is instrumental, you may want to try this arrangement:

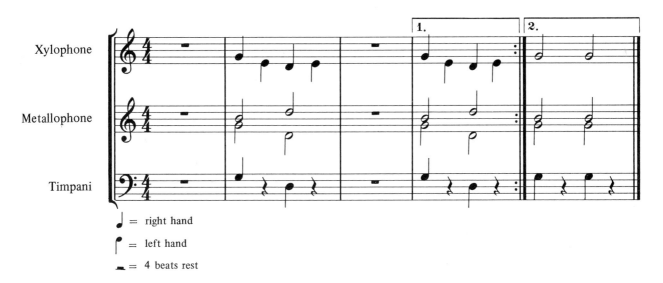

THE COBBLER

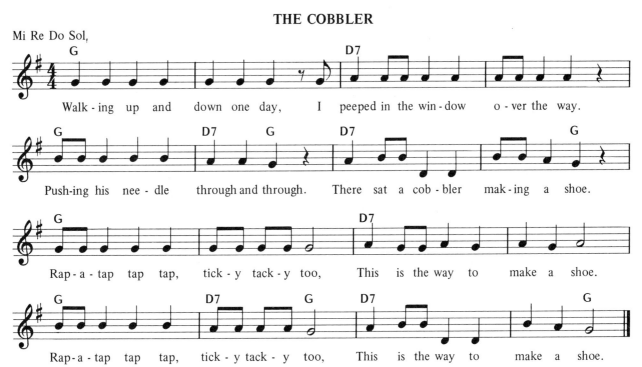

Teaching Suggestions

1. Prepare the class to hear and read the patterns of quarter notes, eighth notes, half notes, and rests with this echo-movement exercise. Ask the students to imitate you. Remember to indicate the beat and tempo before you begin by saying "1-2-3-4."

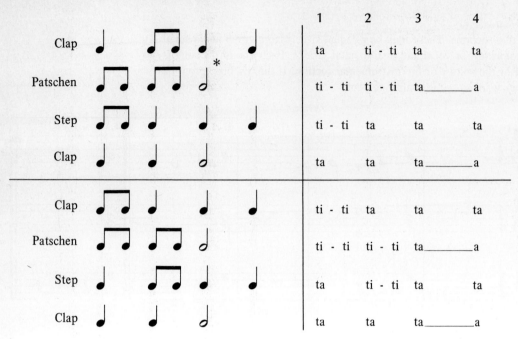

	1	2	3	4
Clap	ta	ti - ti	ta	ta
Patschen	ti - ti	ti - ti	ta_____a	
Step	ti - ti	ta	ta	ta
Clap	ta	ta	ta_____a	
Clap	ti - ti	ta	ta	ta
Patschen	ti - ti	ti - ti	ta_____a	
Step	ta	ti - ti	ta	ta
Clap	ta	ta	ta_____a	

* Make a one-beat motion with your arm to indicate that the note is sustained.

2. Lead the class in reading these patterns, first with durational syllables, then with rhythm instruments.

3. Prepare a color-coded chart so that the students may perform their own accompaniment on autoharp, resonator bells, or guitar. Add rhythm sticks and woodblocks for the section of the song that begins with "Rap-a-tap tap tap."

You will need two chords to accompany this song. Locate the G Major and D₇ bars on the autoharp. Select these tones from your resonator bells.

Guitar Chords

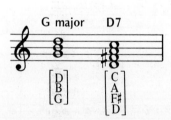

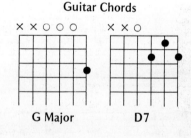

Guitar accompaniment with two chords

Introduction to accompaniment for "The Cobbler"

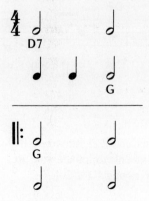

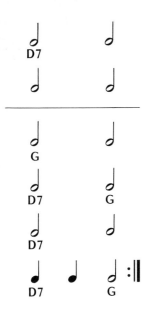

READING AND WRITING PRACTICE: La Sol Mi Re Do

1. Transpose this melody to the staff below it. Sing it and play it on a keyboard. Design a similar exercise for children.

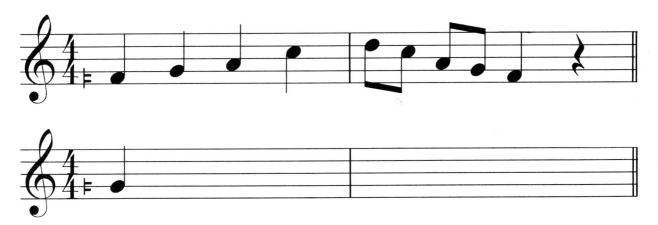

2. Some of the measures in the examples below are incomplete. Write in your choice of rhythmic notation that will provide the beats needed to complete each measure.

3. Write the name of the song that you associate with each melody notated below. Then construct a similar exercise for children using excerpts from the songs you have learned.

HUSH LITTLE BABY

Mi Re Do Sol,

Hush lit - tle ba - by   don't say a word.   Ma-ma's gon-na buy you a   mock - ing bird.

Teaching Suggestions

1. There are many verses to this traditional song. Teach the children several, and then let them create some new ones.

If that mocking bird won't sing,
Mama's gonna buy you a diamond ring.

If that diamond ring turns brass,
Mama's gonna buy you a looking glass.

If that looking glass gets broke,
Mama's gonna buy you a billy goat.

2. Ask the children to select instruments or sound makers to represent the objects in the lyrics. They can add an instrumental variety to this repetitive song.

Glockenspiel

dia - mond ring

Xylophone

look - ing glass

Woodblocks

bil - ly   goat

gliss. – abbreviation for *glissando*

3. Use the song to teach the new interval from *sol₁* to *mi* and *re*. Practice the hand signs for these intervals.

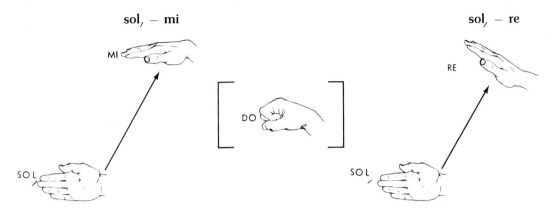

LISTENING AND WRITING PRACTICE: Mi Re Do Sol₁

1. Locate these intervals on your piano and sing them, using the hand signs.

mi   sol₁   do   mi   mi   sol₁   do   mi

2. Sing and play at the keyboard exercise a. Then *transpose,* or move, exercise a from G pentatonic to F pentatonic in b.

HEY, BETTY MARTIN

Mi Re Do La, Sol,

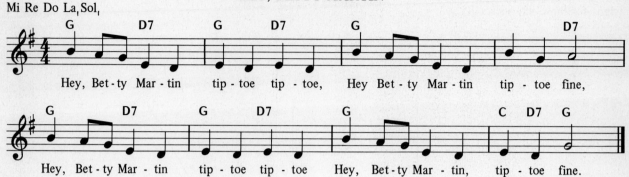

Hey, Bet-ty Mar-tin   tip-toe tip-toe,   Hey Bet-ty Mar-tin   tip-toe fine,

Hey, Bet-ty Mar-tin   tip-toe tip-toe   Hey, Bet-ty Mar-tin,   tip-toe fine.

Teaching Suggestions

1. Show the class the hand signs for *la,*, and *sol,*. Practice singing this pattern with the hand signs.

La, and its hand sign

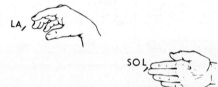

2. Have the class walk in a circle, stepping to the underlying beat of the song. Use the names of children in the class instead of Betty Martin and sing another activity for the class to do.

Movement: a walking circle

Hey, Janice Johnson, reach up reach up;
Hey Janice Johnson, reach up fine.

3. Create a color-coded accompaniment for the class to follow while playing auto-harps.

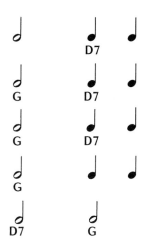

OLD MACDONALD

Mi Re Do La₁ Sol₁

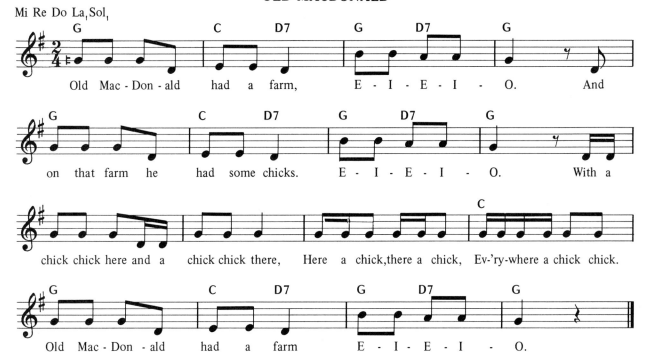

Old Mac - Don - ald   had   a   farm,   E - I - E - I - O.   And

on   that farm   he   had   some chicks.   E - I - E - I - O.   With a

chick chick here and a   chick chick there,   Here   a chick, there a chick,   Ev'ry-where a chick chick.

Old   Mac - Don - ald   had   a   farm   E - I - E - I - O.

Teaching Suggestions

1. Prepare the students to hear, and later read, the internal upbeats which occur with the last half beat in measures 4 and 8. This is also a good song to use for the rote introduction to the sixteenth note and eighth note combinations.

ti   ti - ri   ti - ri - ti

Eighth and sixteenth note combinations

2. Ask the class to clap in imitation of you, placing stress on the first beats. Clap with your class to assist them in their entrance on the upbeat.

3. Use patschen motions on these patterns:

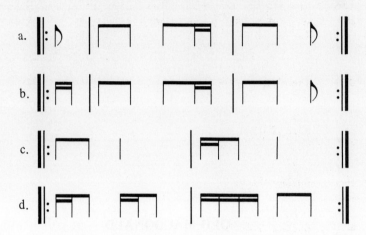

4. Use bells, glockenspiel, or piano on E-I-E-I-O.

E - I - E - I - O

5. Assist a student in using rhythm sticks on:

Chick chick here and a chick chick there,
Here a chick, there a chick, everywhere a chick chick

6. Add several verses by using names of other animals. Vary the arrangements by asking children which instruments to use to depict the animals.

THE HOLE IN THE BUCKET

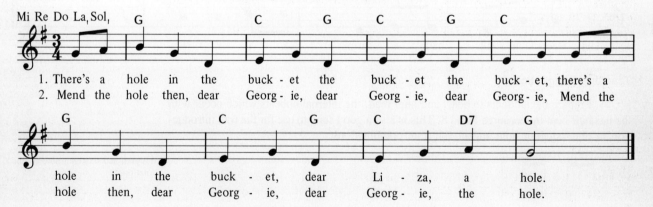

Teacher Preparation

An accompaniment for this song involves rapid chord changes and 3 chords. Locate G Major, C Major, and D$_7$ on your autoharp. Then practice strumming first on the G Major chord in triple meter with strong accents on the first beats. Use the strumming pattern: long-short-short, long-short-short.

Teaching Suggestions

1. Introduce the *do sol la do* melodic pattern. Put the notation on the chalkboard and sing the intervals with the hand signs. Ask the class how many times this pattern occurs in the song.

2. Children enjoy accompanying this humorous country song with movement in triple meter.

>   >   >
stamp clap clap | stamp clap clap | stamp clap clap

DEAR COMPANION

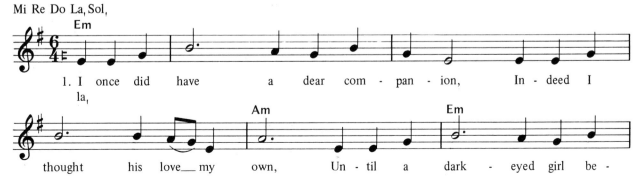

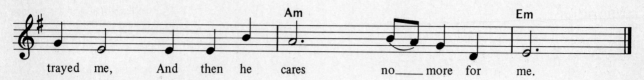

trayed me,   And   then   he   cares   no_____ more for   me.

2. Just go and leave me if you wish to.
   It will never trouble me,
   For in your heart you love another
   And in my grave I'd rather be.

Teacher Preparation

1. The time signature $\frac{6}{4}$ indicates that there are six beats per measure in this song, and that the quarter note equals one beat. Practice counting this way:

Count: 4   5   6   1   2   3   4   5   6   1   2   3   4   5   6

2. "Dear Companion" uses the tones of a natural minor scale, E minor. Minor scales resemble major scales in that they have seven basic tones with an added eighth tone which duplicates the first note an octave higher. Minor scales also resemble major scales through the use of common key signatures. Every major keynote, or home tone (*do*) has a relative minor keynote (*la*). Note in the illustration below that the half steps occur between mi and fa and ti and do in both scales.

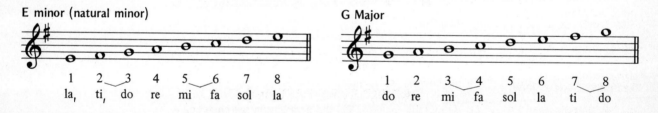

E minor (natural minor)

1   2   3   4   5   6   7   8
la, ti, do   re   mi   fa   sol la

G Major

1   2   3   4   5   6   7   8
do   re   mi   fa   sol la   ti   do

The key signature indicates that F is raised one half step in both E minor and G Major. This alteration creates the half steps between ti and do in E minor, and between ti and do in G Major.

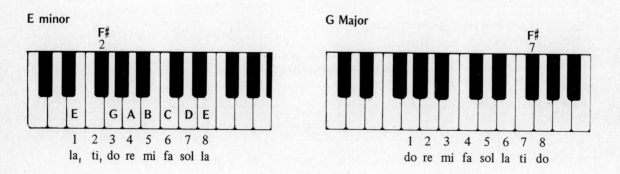

E minor

F#
2

E G A B C D E

1 2 3 4 5 6 7 8
la, ti, do re mi fa sol la

G Major

F#
7

1 2 3 4 5 6 7 8
do re mi fa sol la ti do

3. To accompany the song on the autoharp or guitar you will need to locate the E minor and A minor chords. Strum slowly, three per measure.

PHOEBE IN HER PETTICOAT

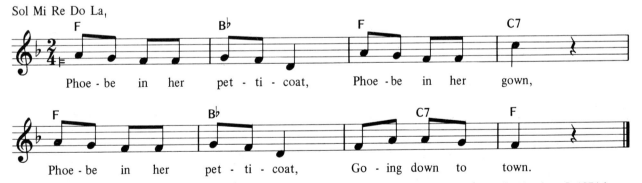

Sol Mi Re Do La,

Phoe - be   in   her   pet - ti - coat,   Phoe - be   in   her   gown,

Phoe - be   in   her   pet - ti - coat,   Go - ing down   to   town.

From *One Hundred Fifty American Folk Songs to Sing, Read and Play* collected by Peter Erdei and Katalin Komlos. © 1974 by Boosey & Hawkes, Inc.

Teaching Suggestions

1. Teach this song by rote. Begin by singing it all the way through for the children. Then ask them to listen carefully as you sing two measures for them. Tell them that you will also listen well as they sing back to you in imitation. Repeat this procedure to the end of the song. Finally, assist the class as they sing the eight measures.

2. Help the children perform this accompaniment with Orff instruments.

Ask a student to highlight the words ''gown'' and ''town'' with a triangle or tone bars on C and F.

3. Use the song to create an inner hearing lesson. Ask the children to step on the beats and sing the first two measures. They should continue stepping to the beats while thinking through the melody and sing again only when they get to the last note on ''town.''

JIM ALONG JOSIE

Sol Mi Re Do La₁

1. Hey jim a-long,___ jim a-long Jo-sie, Hey jim a-long,___ jim a-long Jo.

Hey jim a-long,___ jim a-long Jo-sie, Hey jim a-long,___ jim a-long Jo.

2. Walk jim along, jim along Josie,
   Walk jim along, jim along Jo.
   Walk jim along, jim along Josie,
   Walk jim along, jim along Jo.

3. Hop jim along, jim along Josie,
   Hop jim along, jim along Jo.
   Hop jim along, jim along Josie,
   Hop jim along, jim along Jo.

From *The American Play-Party Song* by B.A. Botkin. Reprinted by permission of the University of Nebraska Press and Mrs. Gertrude Botkin. Copyright 1937.

Teacher Preparation

1. Review the eighth and sixteenth note combinations found in this song.

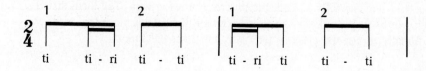

ti　　ti - ri　ti - ti　　ti - ri　ti　ti - ti

2. Write out a rhythm instrument accompaniment using rhythm sticks, woodblocks, drums, and triangles. Assist your methods class in reading the accompaniment from a chart or chalkboard.

3. Prepare a chart showing the rhythm and chord changes for an autoharp accompaniment.

Teaching Suggestion

Ask the children to form a circle for a movement activity. Have them follow the lyrics as they jim (limp), walk, and hop along on this pattern: Ask them to patschen as they move on "jim a-long Jo-sie" and "jim a-long Jo." To give attention to the form of the song, ask them to reverse the direction of their circle after four measures.

TEN LITTLE ANGELS

Sol Mi Re Do La, Sol,

There was one, there were two, there were three lit - tle an - gels, There were

four, there were five, there were six lit - tle an - gels, There were

seven, there were eight, there were nine lit - tle an - gels,

Ten lit - tle an - gels in that band.

Oh was - n't that a band Sun - day mor - ning,

Sun - day morn - ing, Sun - day mor - ning

Was - n't that a band Sun - day mor - ning

Sun - day morn - ing soon.

Teaching Suggestions

1. Use glockenspiel and triangles on the numbers as they occur in the lyrics.

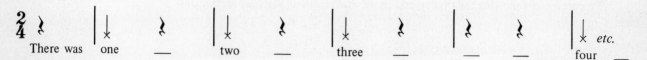

An accompaniment for Orff instruments

2. Have the students prepare an instrumental accompaniment for the chorus of the song, using this arrangement. (16 measures, beginning with "wasn't that a band. . .")

CHATTER WITH THE ANGELS

Teacher Preparation

1. Locate the pentatonic tones of this song on the Orff glockenspiels, xylophones, and metallophones. Write out an accompaniment using simple repeated patterns for children to perform.

2. Develop a rhythm band accompaniment appropriate for the chorus, including resonator bells on B, A, and G to enhance "in that land," "join that band," and "all day long."

Teaching Suggestion

Ask the children to sing the repeated sections on the verse and the chorus very softly. Have them experiment with a crescendo on the last four measures of the song.

READING AND WRITING PRACTICE: Mi Re Do La, Sol,

Write in the notes indicated by the syllables below the staff. Then sing the exercise and play it on the piano.

Syllables	do	sol,	do	re	mi	re	do
Letter names							

Syllables	la,	do	sol,	do	re	mi	do
Letter names							

Compose the solo lines for this rhythm band piece. Perform as soloist with the student teacher group. Then design an exercise of this type for your work with children.

Conduct your piece using the four-beat pattern shown here.

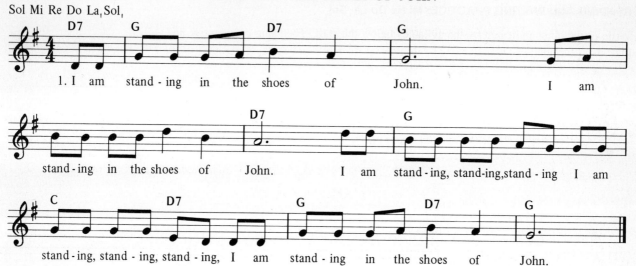

STANDING IN THE SHOES OF JOHN

Sol Mi Re Do La₁ Sol₁

1. I am stand-ing in the shoes of John. I am
stand-ing in the shoes of John. I am stand-ing, stand-ing, stand-ing I am
stand-ing, stand-ing, stand-ing, I am stand-ing in the shoes of John.

2. If they fit me, I will put them on,
   If they fit me, I will put them on,
   If they fit me, fit me, fit me,
   It they fit me, fit me, fit me,
   If they fit me I will put them on.

3. I am going up to get my crown,
   I am going up to get my crown,
   I am going, going, going,
   I am going, going, going,
   I am going up to get my crown.

Teacher Preparation

Prepare a guitar or autoharp accompaniment to assist you in teaching the song. The introduction is intended for presentation before each verse.

Autoharp accompaniment
three chords

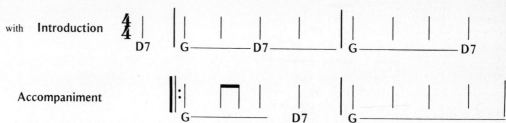

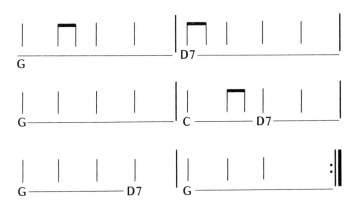

Teaching Suggestion

Develop the students' feeling for the dotted half note, or extended ta (ta-a-a). Ask the children to step or patschen with you 3 times on the 3 beats of "John" each time it occurs. Ask a student to play bells or xylophone on each beat of "John."

Reviewing the dotted half note

MISTER RABBIT

La Sol Mi Re Do Sol,

2. Mister Rabbit, Mister Rabbit, your foot's mighty red,
   "Yes my Lord, I'm almost dead."
   Every little soul must shine, shine,
   Every little soul must shine, shine, shine.

3. Mister Rabbit, Mister Rabbit, your coat's mighty grey,
   "Yes my Lord, 'twas made that way."
   Every little soul must shine, shine,
   Every little soul must shine, shine, shine.

4. Mister Rabbit, Mister Rabbit, your tail's mighty white,
   "Yes my Lord, an' I'm gettin' out o' sight."
   Every little soul must shine, shine,
   Every little soul must shine, shine, shine.

Teacher Preparation

This song, taught by rote, provides reading readiness for dotted note values and syncopation. The teacher should read measure 2 in this way:

ti   ta   ti

Clap 4 ti's. Now clap 1, 2,—, 4, tying 2 and 3. Measures 7 and 8 also feature syncopation:

ti   ta - i

Measures 9, 11, and 13 include dotted quarter notes:

ta   ti - ti = ta   - i - ti = ta - i   ti

Teaching Suggestions

1. Divide the class into two groups, or one group with soloist, and sing the song using this scheme:

Group I: Mister Rabbit, Mister Rabbit, your ear's mighty long,
Group II: Yes, my Lord, they're put on wrong,
All: Ev'ry little soul must shine, shine, shine, *etc.*

2. Use resonator bells or glockenspiel to highlight "shine, shine, shine" at the end of the song.

3. Prepare the students to perform an ostinato accompaniment on Orff instruments.
The preparation for the soprano xylophone requires the teacher to face the class and the students to mirror the motions:

Preparatory motions for an Orff accompaniment

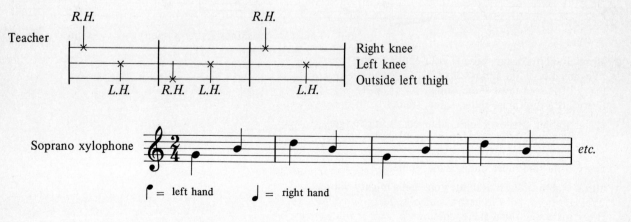

Prepare students to play the alto xylophone ostinato with this exercise:

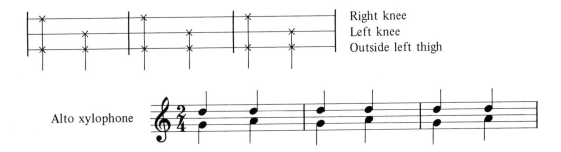

Right knee
Left knee
Outside left thigh

Alto xylophone

Preparation for the metallophone bordun pattern should include these movements:

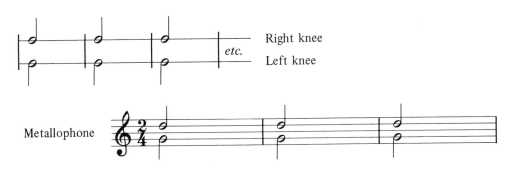

Right knee
Left knee
etc.

Metallophone

THE FARMER IN THE DELL

La Sol Mi Re Do Sol,

The farm - er in the dell, the farm - er in the dell,

Heigh, ho, the Der - ry O, the farm - er in the dell.

2. The farmer takes a wife,
   The farmer takes a wife,
   Heigh, ho, the Derry O,
   The farmer takes a wife.

3. The wife takes the child,
   The wife takes the child,
   Heigh, ho, the Derry O,
   The wife takes the child.

4. The child takes the nurse,
   The child takes the nurse,
   Heigh, ho, the Derry O,
   The child takes the nurse.

5. The nurse takes the dog,
   The nurse takes the dog,
   Heigh, ho, the Derry O,
   The nurse takes the dog.

6. The dog takes the cat,
   The dog takes the cat,
   Heigh, ho, the Derry O,
   The dog takes the cat.

7. The cat takes the rat,
   The cat takes the rat,
   Heigh, ho, the Derry O,
   The cat takes the rat.

8. The rat takes the cheese.
   The rat takes the cheese,
   Heigh, ho, the Derry O,
   The rat takes the cheese.

9. The cheese stands alone,
   The cheese stands alone,
   Heigh, ho, the Derry O,
   The cheese stands alone.

Teacher Preparation

The teacher's reading skills should include meters such as $\frac{6}{8}$ in which the beat unit is the eighth note.

Note that values in $\frac{6}{8}$ for this song are:

♪ = 1

♩ = 2

♩. = 3

𝄾. = 3

The accents here fall on beats 1 and 4, **1** 2 3 **4** 5 6, giving the feeling of **1——2——**, or *duple meter*.

Teaching Suggestions

1. Use a different melodic or percussion instrument on "Heigh, ho, the Derry O" for each verse. Ask the class to suggest instruments. These might include resonator bells, glockenspiel, or xylophone on the notes of the line.
   Rhythm sticks, woodblocks, temple blocks, and hand drums may be used to play the rhythm of the lyrics.

Circle dance in $\frac{6}{8}$ time

2. Have the class form a circle, join hands, and move alternately counterclockwise and clockwise, changing for each verse. One student is "the farmer in the dell" and moves inside the group in the opposite direction. On verse 2 he "takes a wife" and they both move in the opposite direction of the outside group. In verse 3, the farmer steps back into the main circle and "the wife takes the child." These partners then move inside the circle. The pattern is repeated until verse 9, in which the "cheese stands alone" inside the circle.

Playing and Improvising in $\frac{6}{8}$

Arranged by R. Herrold

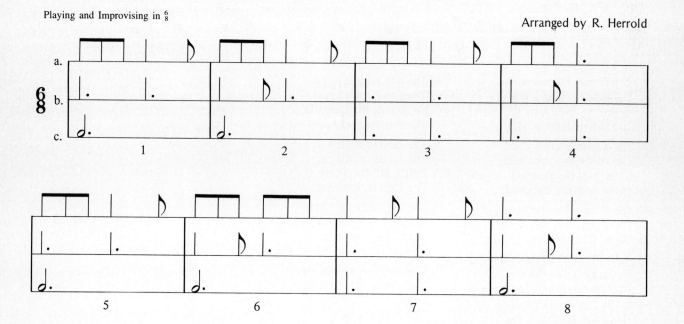

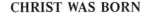

Teaching Suggestions

1. Express the rhythm in movement. Divide the class into three groups and assign three different motions for performance of the parts.

2. Transfer the movement to rhythm band ensemble parts.

3. Try pentatonic *improvisation* on the rhythms. Locate the bars corresponding to the C pentatonic scale on the Orff instruments. Remove the others. Perform the rhythm of the *a* section on the glockenspiel, and the rhythms of the *b* and *c* sections on xylophones and metallophones. Allow freedom and random selection in creating melodies from known rhythms. *Improvisation* is creating and performing music simultaneously.

4. Ask the class to complete measures 9–16. Select some of the student compositions for the class to perform.

CHRIST WAS BORN

La Sol Mi Re Do La,

2. Son of Mary, Lord is He,
   Christ was born in Bethlehem.
   Son of Mary, Lord is he,
   Came to save us all from sin.

Teacher Preparation

1. Practice an autoharp or guitar accompaniment using these chords:

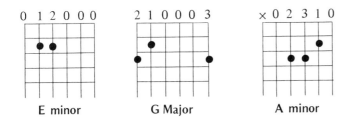

If you use the autoharp, strum over all the strings on beat 1, and over the middle area of the strings for beats 2 and 3.

When playing the accompaniment on guitar, use your thumb to pluck the lowest tone on beat 1 of each measure. Then strum down over the other strings on beats 2 and 3 of each measure, using the fingernails of fingers 2 and 3.

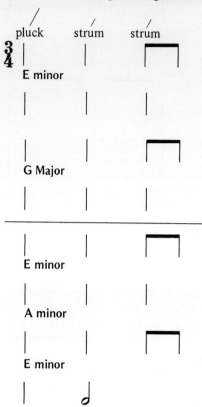

2. Practice the conducting pattern diagrammed below. Note that the preparatory gesture here must precede the upbeat, which falls on the words "Christ was."

Conducting the three-beat pattern

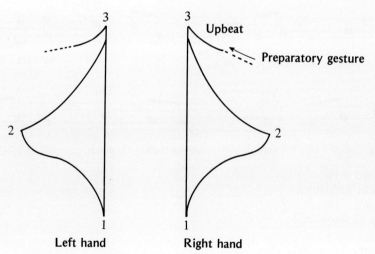

Teaching Suggestions

To lengthen and add variety to this brief, beautiful carol, ask the class to hum a verse or to sing on the syllable "loo." Use glockenspiel, melody bells, or resonator bells to enhance the first beat in each measure.

MARY HAD A BABY

La Sol Mi Re Do La, Sol,

Ma - ry had a ba - by, yes, Lord. Ma - ry had a ba - by,

yes my Lord. Ma - ry had a ba - by, yes, Lord. The

peo - ple keep - a com - in' an' the train's done gone.

Teaching Suggestions

1. Try this spiritual with two groups in a statement-answer format.

Group I:	Mary had a ba-by.
Group II:	Yes, Lord.
Group I:	Mary had a ba-by.
Group II:	Yes, My Lord.
Group I:	Mary had a baby.
Group II:	Yes, Lord.
All:	The people keep-a comin an' the train's done gone.

2. This is a good song to use for introducing or reinforcing the *do-la*₁ and *do-la*₁*-sol* intervals. Sing the melodic syllables for the first measure to the class (*do do do do re mi*) and have the class answer do-sol₁. Demonstrate the hand signs for the interval *do-sol,* and *do-la*₁*-sol*₁.

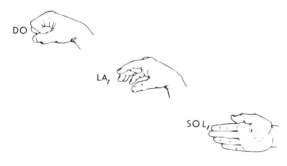

3. Autoharp accompaniment:

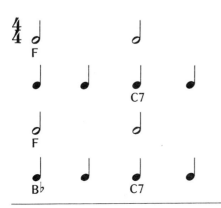

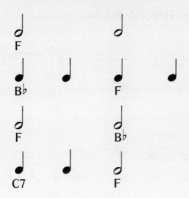

4. Practice the additional verses.

2. What did she name him, yes, Lord.
   What did she name him, yes my Lord.
   What did she name him, yes Lord.
   The people keep a-comin' an' the train's done gone.

3. Named him King Jesus, yes, Lord.
   Named him King Jesus, yes my Lord.
   Named him King Jesus, yes Lord.
   The people keep a-comin' an' the train's done gone.

4. Where was he born, yes, Lord.
   Where was he born, yes my Lord.
   Where was he born, yes Lord.
   The people keep a-comin' an' the train's done gone.

5. Born in a manger, yes Lord.
   Born in a manger, yes my Lord.
   Born in a manger, yes Lord.
   The people keep a-comin' an' the train's done gone.

5. Use glockenspiel or resonator bells on "yes, Lord" in measure 2 (*do-sol₁*), on "yes, my Lord" in measure 4 (*do-la₁-sol₁*) and on "yes, Lord" in measure 6 (*la-sol*).

6. Make changes in the presentations of the various verses. Ask the class for suggestions. They may want to experiment with the following ideas: 1) soloist with the group answering, 2) dynamic changes within a verse or contrasting dynamics from one verse to another, 3) an Orff instrumentarium accompaniment on one of the verses.

SAILING ON THE OCEAN

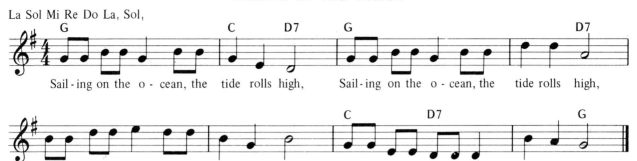

La Sol Mi Re Do La, Sol,

Sail-ing on the o - cean, the tide rolls high, Sail-ing on the o - cean, the tide rolls high,

Sail-ing on the o - cean, the tide rolls high, You can get a pret-ty girl, by and by.

2. Got me a pretty girl, stay all day,
   Got me a pretty girl, stay all day,
   Got me a pretty girl, stay all day,
   We don't care what the others say.

3. Eight in the boat and it won't go 'round,
   Eight in the boat and it won't go 'round,
   Eight in the boat and it won't go 'round,
   You can have the pretty girl you just found.

Teacher Preparation

sol,	la,	do	re	mi	sol	la
D	E	G	A	B	D	E

Practice the hand signs for the intervals in measures 2 and 4. Locate these notes on the piano or resonator bells.

Teaching Suggestions

1. Children can prepare a simple ostinato pentatonic accompaniment on Orff instruments using the following scheme:

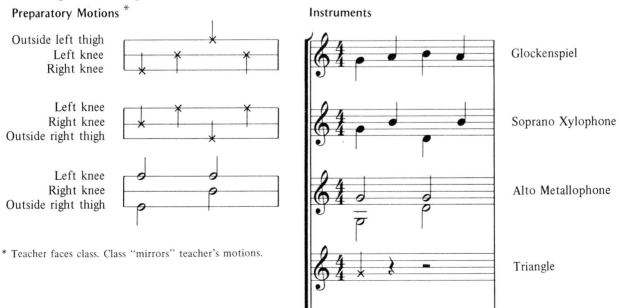

* Teacher faces class. Class "mirrors" teacher's motions.

2. Locate three chords on the resonator bells and autoharp. Prepare a color-coded accompaniment chart which displays the rhythm and the chord changes.
Resonator Bells:

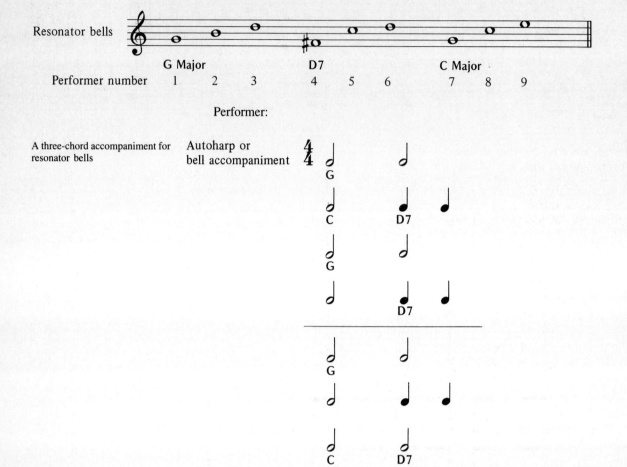

Resonator bells

G Major   D7   C Major

Performer number   1   2   3   4   5   6   7   8   9

Performer:

A three-chord accompaniment for resonator bells

Autoharp or bell accompaniment

TURN THE GLASSES OVER

La Sol Mi Re Do La, Sol,

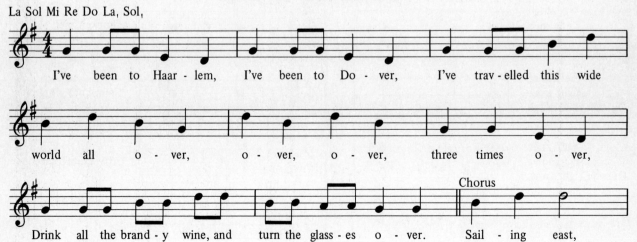

I've been to Haar-lem,   I've been to Do-ver,   I've trav-elled this wide

world all o-ver,   o-ver,   o-ver,   three times o-ver,

Drink all the brand-y wine, and   turn the glass-es o-ver.   Sail-ing east,

sail - ing west,   Sail - ing o'er the   o - cean,   Bet-ter watch out when the

boat be - gins to rock,   or   you'll lose your girl   in the   o - cean.

Teaching Suggestions

1. Use sections of this song for a review of reading skills. Show the class the hand signs for low la, and sol,.

On a chart or the chalkboard write these patterns:

	1	2	3	4
Melody	d	d d	l,	s,
Rhythm	ta	ti - ti	ta	ta

Melody	d	d d	m m	s s	m m	r r	d	d
Rhythm	ta	ti - ti	ti - ti	ti - ti	ti - ti	ti - ti	ta	ta

2. Children can perform this simple accompaniment with autoharps from a color-coded chart. The song is more attractive when color is added through special instrumental parts for rhythm instruments and bells.

Autoharp **4/4**

    G   D7   I've been to Haarlem,

    G   D7   I've been to Dover,

    G   I've travelled this wide

                    World all over.

𝅗𝅥 G	𝅗𝅥 G	Over, over,
𝅗𝅥 C	𝅗𝅥 D7	Three times over,
𝅗𝅥 G	𝅗𝅥 G	Drink all the brandy wine, and
𝅗𝅥 D7	𝅗𝅥 G	Turn the glasses over.

𝅗𝅥 G	𝅗𝅥 G	Sailing east,
𝅗𝅥 G	𝅗𝅥 G	Sailing west,
𝅗𝅥 G	𝅗𝅥 G	Sailing o'er the
𝅗𝅥 D7	𝅗𝅥 D7	O-cean,

𝅗𝅥 G	♩ C	♩ D7	Better watch out when the
𝅗𝅥 G	♩ C	♩ D7	Boat begins to rock, or
𝅗𝅥 G	𝅗𝅥 G		You'll lose your girl in the
𝅗𝅥 D7	𝅗𝅥 G		O-cean.

3. Use glockenspiel or resonator bells on "Sailing east, sailing west, sailing o'er the ocean."

4. Use a rocking motion appropriate for the last two lines. Use rhythm sticks on the pattern ♫ | ♩ | 𝄽 , "better watch out." Continue this pattern to the end of the song.

MISTER FROG WENT A-COURTING

La Sol Mi Re Do, La, Sol,

Mis - ter   Frog   went   a - court - ing,   he   did   ride,   ah - hah,   ah -

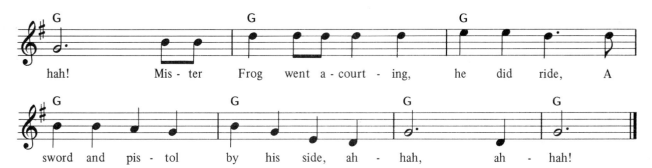

hah!   Mis - ter   Frog   went a - court - ing,   he   did   ride,   A

sword   and   pis - tol   by   his   side,   ah - hah,   ah - hah!

2. He rode up to Miss Mousie's den,
   Ah-hah, ah-hah!
   He rode up to Miss Mousie's den,
   He said, "Miss Mouse, are you within?"
   Ah-hah, ah-hah!

3. "Oh, Mister Frog, I sit and spin,"
   Ah-hah, ah-hah!
   "Oh, Mister Frog, I sit and spin,
   Just lift the latch and please come in."
   Ah-hah, ah-hah!

4. He took Miss Mousie on his knee,
   Ah-hah, ah-hah!
   He took Miss Mousie on his knee,
   He said, "Miss Mouse, will you marry me?"
   Ah-hah, ah-hah!

5. "Without my Uncle Rat's consent,"
   Ah-hah, ah-hah!
   "Without my Uncle Rat's consent,
   I wouldn't marry the President."
   Ah-hah, ah-hah!

6. Now Uncle Rat when he came home
   Ah-hah, ah-hah!
   Now Uncle Rat when he came home
   Says, "Who's been here since I been gone?"
   Ah-hah, ah-hah!

7. "A very fine gentleman has been here
   Ah-hah, ah-hah!
   "A very fine gentleman has been here
   Who wishes me to be his dear."
   Ah-hah, ah-hah!

8. So Uncle Rat he went to town
   Ah-hah, ah-hah!
   So Uncle Rat he went to town
   To buy his niece a wedding-gown.
   Ah-hah, ah-hah!

9. Where will the wedding supper be?
   Ah-hah, ah-hah!
   Where will the wedding supper be?
   Away down yonder in a hollow tree.
   Ah-hah, ah-hah!

10. What will the wedding supper be?
    Ah-hah, ah-hah!
    What will the wedding supper be?
    Two green beans and a black-eyed pea.
    Ah-hah, ah-hah!

11. They all went a-sailing on the lake,
    Ah-hah, ah-hah!
    They all went a-sailing on the lake,
    They all were swallowed by a big black snake.
    Ah-hah, ah-hah!

12. So there's the end of one, two, three:
    Ah-hah, ah-hah!
    So there's the end of one, two, three:
    The Rat, the Frog, and Miss Mousie.
    Ah-hah, ah-hah!

13. There's bread and cheese upon the shelf;
    Ah-hah, ah-hah!
    There's bread and cheese upon the shelf;
    If you want any more, you can sing it yourself.
    Ah-hah, ah-hah!

Teaching Suggestions

1. Try this scheme with Orff instruments on ostinato patterns:

2. This song lends itself to an easy autoharp accompaniment that the class members can play using just the G Major chord bar, strumming on the first beat of each measure.

LISTENING AND COMPOSITION PRACTICE: La Sol Mi Re Do La₁ Sol₁

1. Number these rhythm patterns in the order they are performed for you.

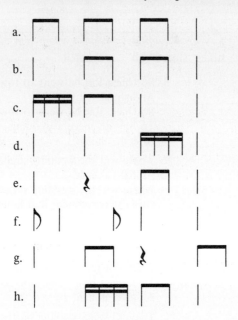

2. Create a melody for the rhythm indicated below. Use the syllables *la, sol, mi, re, do, la₁,* and *sol₁.* (Letter names in G pentatonic would be E, D, B, A, G, E, and D₁.)

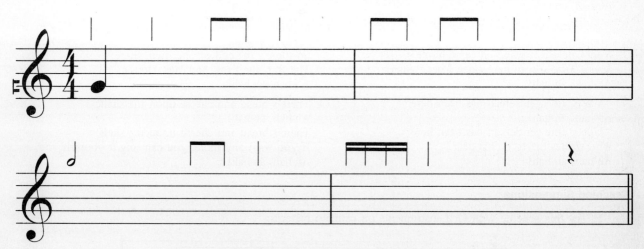

3. Write your melody for the class. Find the starting pitch on the pitch pipe or piano, and lead the group in reading your composition.

COTTON NEEDS PICKIN'

La Sol Mi Re Do La₁ Sol₁
Chorus

Cot-ton needs pick-in'   so   bad,   cot-ton needs pick-in'   so   bad.___

Cot-ton needs pick-in', so bad I'm gon-na pick all o-ver this field. *Fine*

Plant-ed this cot-ton in A - pril, On the full of the moon, It's

been a hot dry sum - mer, That's why it o-pened so soon. *D.C. al Fine*

Teacher Preparation

A five-chord autoharp accompaniment featuring strums on beats 1 and 3 of each measure assists the class in keeping a steady beat throughout this syncopated song.

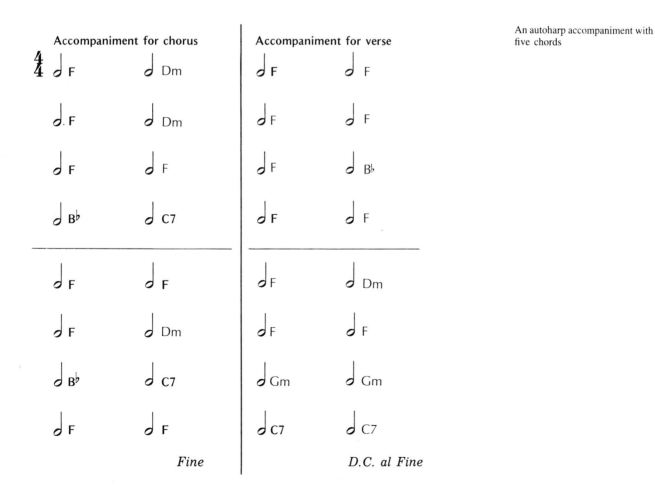

Accompaniment for chorus

Accompaniment for verse

An autoharp accompaniment with five chords

DOWN IN A VALLEY

La Sol Mi Re Do La, Sol,

Down   in   a   val - ley,   Sing   hal - le - lu,
Mary   had   a   ba - by,   Sing   hal - le - lu,

Down   in   a   val - ley,   Sing   hal - le - lu.
Mary   had   a   ba - by,   Sing   hal - le - lu.

Down   in   a   val - ley,   Sing   hal - le - lu.
Mary   had   a   ba - by,   Sing   hal - le - lu.

Down   in   a   val - ley,   Sing   hal - le - lu.
Mary   had   a   ba - by,   Sing   hal - le - lu.

Teacher Preparation

The dotted eighth followed by a sixteenth note may be derived as follows:

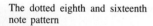
The dotted eighth and sixteenth note pattern

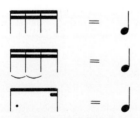

The methods class can practice ⌐· ⌐ by having one group tap ⊓⊓⊓ | and another group simultaneously tap ⌐· ⌐ |.

Teaching Suggestions

The repetitious nature of this song allows students to focus their attention on aspects of form and experiment with dynamic contrasts.

1. Try a call-and-response style with two groups:

Group I: Down in a valley *p*
Group II: Sing hallelu *f*
Group I: Down in a valley *p*
Group II: Sing hallelu *f*
                    etc.

2. Select four students to play resonator bells, glockenspiel, or xylophone on the syncopated patterns.

Performing syncopated patterns

mm. 3, 4   mm. 11, 12

mm. 7, 8   mm. 15, 16

3. Ask the students to identify the lines of the song that have the same rhythmic features. Then ask them if the melody is repeated in each line, and if the melodic contour is similar.

OLD TEXAS

La Sol Mi Re Do La, Sol,

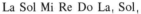

I'm goin' to leave_____ old___ Tex - as   now.

They've got   no   use_____ for the long - horn   cow. _____

2. They've plowed and fenced my cattle range,
And the people there are all so strange.

3. I'll take my horse, I'll take my rope,
And hit the trail upon a lope.

4. Say adios to the Alamo
And hit the trail toward Mexico.

Teacher Preparation

Prepare a guitar accompaniment using the F Major and C_7 chords.

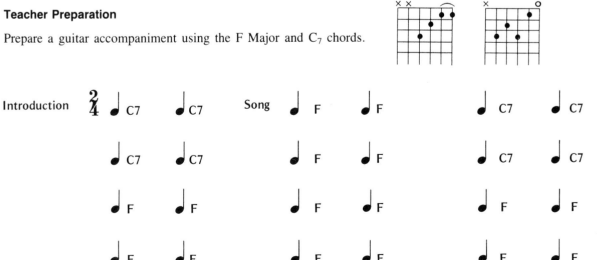

Teaching Suggestions

1. This song is frequently performed with two parts, with the second group echoing the first during the sustained notes.

A two-part echo song

Group I: I'm goin' to leave _____
Group II: _____ I'm goin' to leave
Group I: Old Texas now. _____
Group II: _____ Old Texas now.
Group I: They've got no use _____
Group II: _____ They've got no use
Group I: For the longhorn cow. _____
Group II: _____ For the longhorn cow.

2. Use resonator bells on "leave," "now," "use," and "cow."

READING AND WRITING PRACTICE: Melodic Contour

1. Number these melodies in the order they are performed for you. Note that they all begin on *do*.

2. Now go back and sing the four examples. Use syllables, scale numbers, or letter names as you practice.

3. Write the melodic and rhythmic notation that corresponds to this shorthand:

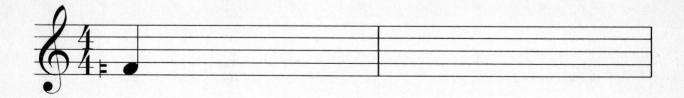

DANCE JOSEY

La Sol Mi Re Do La, Sol,

Chick-en in the fence post,   can't dance Jo - sey,   Chick-en in the fence post,   can't dance Jo - sey,

Chick-en in the fence post,   can't dance Jo - sey,   Hel - lo Su - san   Brown - y - o.

2. Choose your partner and come dance Josey, *(Sing 3 times)*
   Hello Susan Browny-o.

3. Chew my gum while I dance Josey, *(Sing 3 times)*
   Hello Susan Browny-o.

4. Shoestring's broke and I can't dance Josey, *(Sing 3 times)*
   Hello Susan Browny-o.

5. Hold my mule while I dance Josey, *(Sing 3 times)*
   Hello Susan Browny-o.

Teaching Suggestions

1. Prepare the class for the sixteenth note pattern through motion and in aural work. The children achieve reading readiness through such experiences.

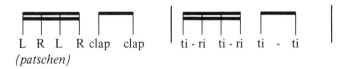

L   R   L   R clap   clap   ti - ri ti - ri ti - ti
(patschen)

2. *Line Dance:* Have the class form two parallel lines. The partners face one another to begin the dance.

> *Verse 1:* All dancers use one foot to stamp and hands to clap on the beat.   A parallel line dance
> *Verse 2:* Partners link right arms and swing clockwise.
> *Verse 3:* All dancers "chew gum" while standing in place and bending at the knees on beat 2 of each measure.
> *Verse 4:* One line "hobbles" in place on the beat while their partners skip around to form a new line behind them.
> *Verse 5:* The newly formed line "holds" the reins on their "mules" while their partners step on the beats around them (individually).

3. The song can be accompanied by children, using the G Major chord on the beats. This is a good positive experience for students who may have difficulty with chord changes.

CRAWDAD

2. Get up old man, you slept too late, honey/babe, (*Repeat*)
   Get up old man, you slept too late,
   Last piece of crawdad's on your plate,
   Honey, sugar-baby mine.

3. Get up old woman, you slept too late, honey/babe, (*Repeat*)
   Get up old woman, you slept too late,
   Crawdad man done passed your gate,
   Honey, sugar-baby mine.

4. Along come a man with a sack on his back, honey/babe, (*Repeat*)
   Along come a man with a sack on his back,
   Packin' all the crawdads he can pack,
   Honey, sugar-baby mine.

5. What you gonna do when the lake goes dry, honey/babe? (*Repeat*)
   What you gonna do when the lake goes dry,
   Sit on the bank and watch the crawdads die,
   Honey, sugar-baby mine.

6. What you gonna do when the crawdads die, honey/babe? (*Repeat*)
   What you gonna do when the crawdads die,
   Sit on the bank until I cry,
   Honey, sugar-baby mine.

7. I heard the duck say to the drake, honey/babe, (*Repeat*)
   I heard the duck say to the drake,
   There ain't no crawdads in this lake,
   Honey, sugar-baby mine.

* "Blues" note: See Glossary

Teacher Preparation

Prepare a guitar or autoharp accompaniment using G Major, D₇, and C Major chords:

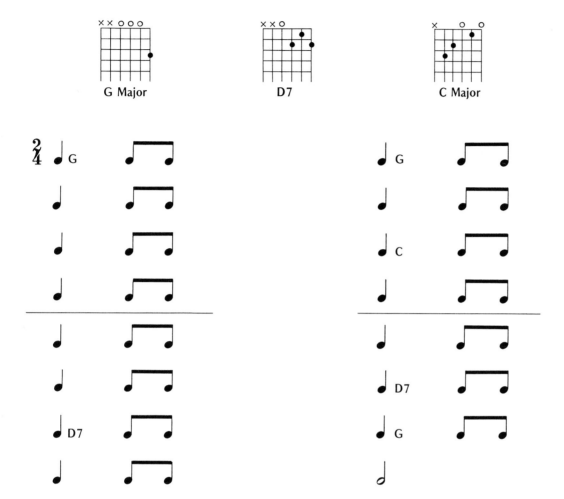

Teaching Suggestions

1. Select a group to echo "honey," "babe," and "mine," on the sustained notes (measures 4, 8, and 16).

2. Divide the class into two groups. Have each group perform a movement accompaniment.

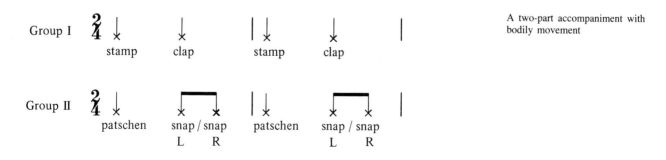

A two-part accompaniment with bodily movement

3. Write these rhythmic patterns on the chalkboard to assist the children in understanding the eighth/sixteenth note figure which is a feature of this song.

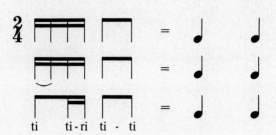

ti   ti - ri   ti - ti

Ask one group to tap [pattern], while another taps [pattern], and a third taps the new pattern [pattern].

4. To explain the syncopation in measures 3 and 13, write this sequence.

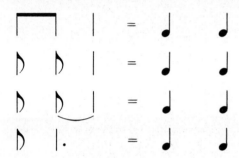

THE CHERRY TREE CAROL

La Sol Mi Re Do La, Sol,

Jo - seph were a young man, a young man were he, And he

court - ed Vir - gin Mar - y, the____ Queen of Gal - i - lee, And he

court - ed Vir - gin Mar - y, the____ Queen of Gal - i - lee.

2. Mary and Joseph were a-walking one day,
   "Here is apples and cherries a-plenty to behold.
   Here is apples and cherries a-plenty to behold."

3. Mary spoke to Joseph so meek and so mild,
   "Joseph, gather me some cherries for I am with child,
   Joseph, gather me some cherries for I am with child."

Teaching Suggestions

1. Lead the class in an echo-clapping exercise to develop an awareness of the dotted quarter note duration.

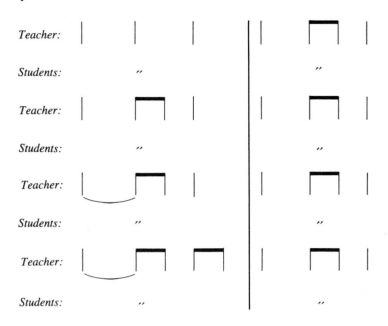

2. Select students to perform these ostinato patterns on Orff instruments for a simple accompaniment.

3. An autoharp accompaniment, with chord changes indicated in colors, can be performed by young players.

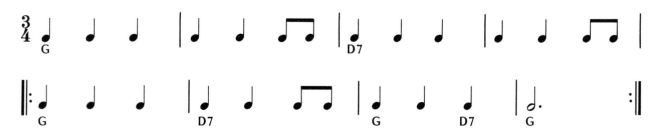

SWING LOW, SWEET CHARIOT

2. Swing low, sweet chariot
   Coming for to carry me home
   Swing low, sweet chariot
   Coming for to carry me home.
   If you get there before I do
   Coming for to carry me home
   Just tell my friends I'm coming too
   Coming for to carry me home.

3. Swing low, sweet chariot
   Coming for to carry me home
   Swing low, sweet chariot
   Coming for to carry me home.
   I'm sometimes up and sometimes down
   Coming for to carry me home
   But still my soul feels heavenly bound
   Coming for to carry me home.

Teacher Preparation

The rhythm in measures 2, 6, 10, and 14 may be derived from this sequence. Practice the new rhythm by tapping or clapping the patterns.

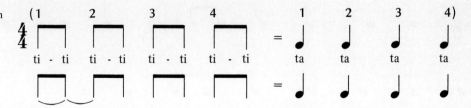

Studying syncopation in notation

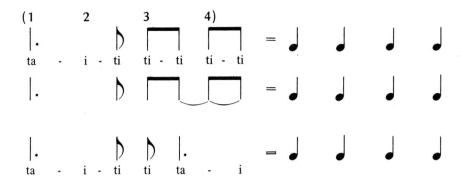

The rhythm in measure 9 may be practiced in this sequence:

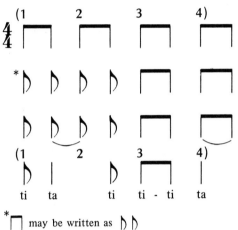

*⊓ may be written as ♪ ♪

Teaching Suggestions

1. Try the song as a canon.

Group I: Swing low sweet chariot Coming for to carry me   home.
Group II: _____ Swing low _____ sweet chariot.

2. Movement accompaniment:

4/4 ↓   ↓   ↓   ↓ |
     x   x   x   x
     tap   clap   tap   clap
     foot   foot

4/4 ↓   ↓   ↓   ↓ |
     x   x   x   x
     patschen snap patschen snap

3. Ostinato patterns performed on Orff and rhythm instruments provide an easy accompaniment for this favorite spiritual.

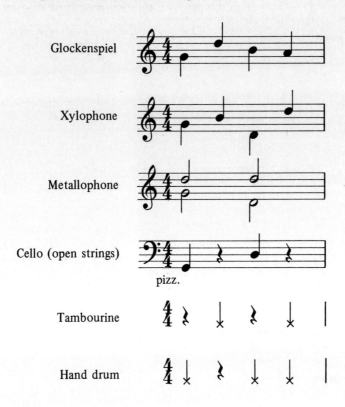

READING AND WRITING PRACTICE: Rhythmic Notation and Canon

1. Some of the measures below are incomplete. Write in any combination of notes that will give them the required number of beats. Then write out an exercise of your own design.

2. Play this exercise on rhythm sticks. Perform as a canon, with the second group beginning after the first group has completed a measure.

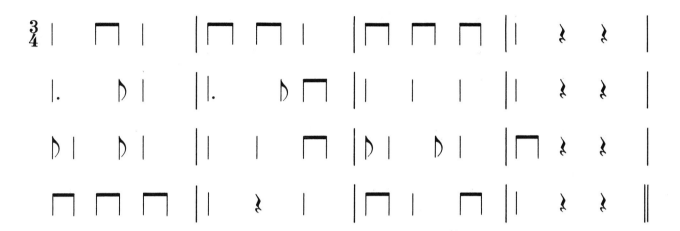

GO TELL IT ON THE MOUNTAIN

La Sol Mi Re Do La, Sol,

1. When I was a seek - er, I sought both night and day; I asked the Lord to help me, And He showed me the way.

Chorus
Go tell it on the moun - tains, O - ver the hills and ev - ery - where;
Go tell it on the moun - tains that Je - sus Christ is born.

2. He made me a watchman upon the city wall,
   And if I serve Him truly, I am the least of all.

3. In the time of David some said he was a king,
   And if a child is true born, the Lord will hear him sing.

Teacher Preparation

1. Learn to read the dotted eighth/sixteenth note combinations in this song by tapping and clapping this sequence:

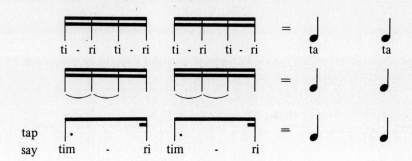

Now practice saying the durational syllables.

2. Practice reading the syncopated rhythms in measures 11 and 15 by clapping and chanting the durational syllables of these patterns:

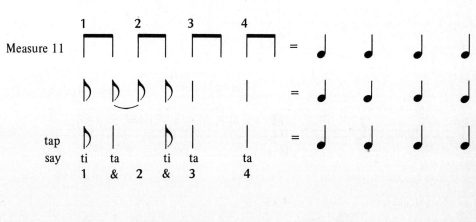

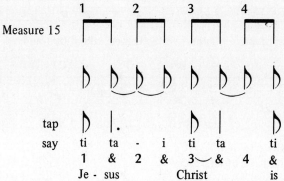

Teaching Suggestions

1. Assist the class in reading the verse of the song. Write *do* on the staff.

Placement of a beginning pitch

do   mi

Ask the class to find the placement of the beginning pitch (*mi*). Ask class members to locate the interval *do-mi* on the piano and resonator bells.

Review intervals with the class. Write them on the chalkboard and point to them for the class to sing, first in order from left to right, then in reverse, and finally in random order. Include sequences from the song.

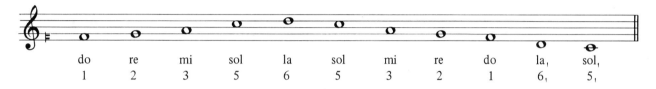

do	re	mi	sol	la	sol	mi	re	do	la,	sol,
1	2	3	5	6	5	3	2	1	6,	5,

2. Write out a color-coded chart indicating the rhythm of the accompaniment and the chord changes. Suggested colors are F Major = blue, B♭ Major = green, and C₇ = red.

Try using resonator bells with one player for each chord tone on the verse. Change to guitar or autoharp accompaniment on the chorus.

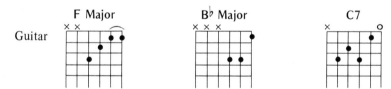

Guitar

F Major   B♭ Major   C7

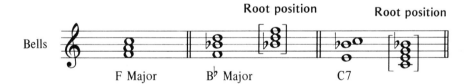

Bells

    F Major   B♭ Major   C7

Root position   Root position

Guitar or autoharp accompaniment:

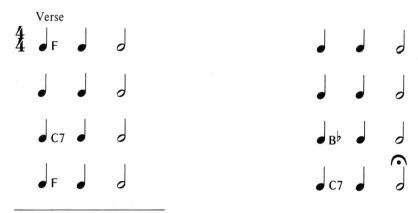

Verse

WAYFARING STRANGER

La Sol Mi Re Do La, Sol,

I'm just a poor way-far-in' strang-er, A trav-lin' thru this world of woe. And there's no sick-ness, toil, or dan-ger, In that far land to which I go. I'm go-in' there to see my Fa-ther, I'm go-in' there no more to roam. I'm just a-go-in' o-ver Jor-dan, I'm just a-go-in' o-ver home.

Teacher Preparation

1. Read the upbeat, or anacrusis, as 1½ beats coming before the first complete measure of 3 beats.

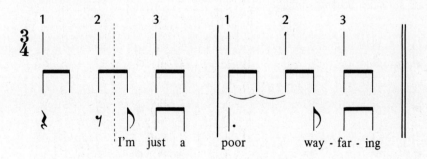

2. Practice strumming the E minor and A minor chords on your guitar to provide a simple accompaniment for this plaintive song. Try the following approach:

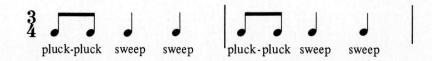

Thumb on root of chord (marked R)

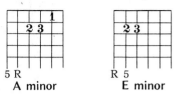

A minor   E minor

CINDY

Teaching Suggestions

1. Use a bodily movement and rhythm instrument accompaniment for the verse. An autoharp accompaniment works well with the chorus here. Remember to give the correct starting pitch for the verse!

Creating an accompaniment with bodily movement

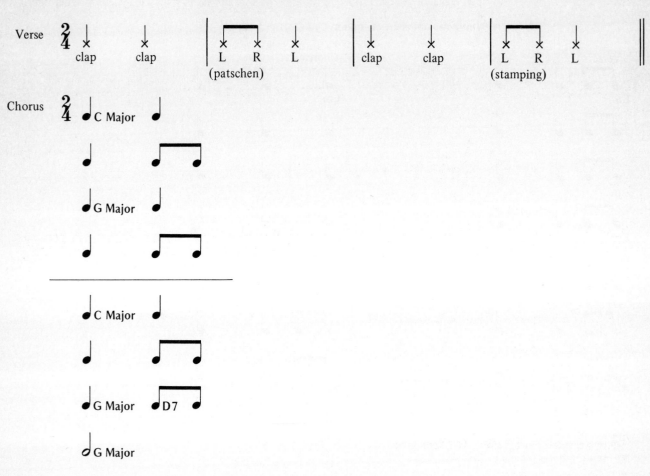

2. Try this simple *descant* on the chorus:

LIZA JANE

Do' La Sol Mi Re Do

1.Come my love and go with me, Li'l Li - za Jane,

Come my love and go with me, Li'l Li - za Jane.

O, E - li - za! Li'l Li - za Jane,

O, E - li - za! Li'l Li - za Jane.

2. I've got a house in Baltimore, Li'l Liza Jane,
   Street car runs right by my door, Li'l Liza Jane.
   O, Eliza, Li'l Liza Jane.
   O, Eliza, Li'l Liza Jane.

3. I've got a house in Baltimore, Li'l Liza Jane,
   Brussels carpet on the floor, Li'l Liza Jane.
   O, Eliza, Li'l Liza Jane.
   O, Eliza, Li'l Liza Jane.

4. I've got a house in Baltimore, Li'l Liza Jane,
   Silver doorplate on the door, Li'l Liza Jane.
   O, Eliza, Li'l Liza Jane.
   O, Eliza, Li'l Liza Jane.

Teaching Suggestions

1. Use this song to review the durational syllables and notation for syncopation. Incorporate syncopated patterns from the song into an echo-clapping exercise before introducing the song.

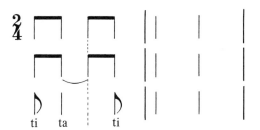

ti ta ti

2. Use a movement ostinato with patschen throughout the song. Divide the group into two sections: one section performs patschen on the beats, the other group performs the syncopated pattern simultaneously.

3. Sing the song as a round, with the entrance of the second group after one measure is sung by the first section.

4. Use simple percussion instruments on the syncopated pattern each time it is sung ("Li'l Liza Jane").

5. Use song bells on "Li'l Liza Jane." Two performers: one with AGEG and one with EDC.

A circle dance   6. Sketch out a simple circle dance to be performed as the song is sung 3 times. Remember to change directions only after 8 measures are completed. (You'll need 6 directions in all.)

READING AND WRITING PRACTICE: The Octave

1. Practice reading and singing the high *do'* in octaves.

2. Sing *do-sol* (fifth) and *sol-do'* (fourth). In scale numbers these intervals correspond to 1-5, 5-8.

3. Write in the notes indicated by syllable names below the staff.

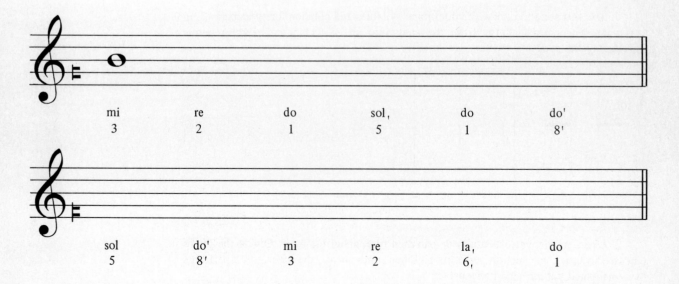

mi	re	do	sol,	do	do'
3	2	1	5	1	8'

sol	do'	mi	re	la,	do
5	8'	3	2	6,	1

RIDING IN THE BUGGY

Do' La Sol Mi Re Do

2. Sally's got a house in Baltimore
   In Baltimore, in Baltimore.
   Sally's got a house in Baltimore
   And it's full of chicken pie.
   Who moans for me,
   Who moans for me,
   Who moans for me, my darling,
   Who moans for me?

3. I've got a girl in Baltimore
   In Baltimore, in Baltimore,
   I've got a girl in Baltimore
   And she's sixteen stories high.
   Who moans for me,
   Who moans for me,
   Who moans for me, my darling,
   Who moans for me?

4. Fare you well, my little bitty Ann,
   Little bitty Ann, little bitty Ann,
   Fare you well, my little bitty Ann,
   For I'm going away.
   Who moans for me,
   Who moans for me,
   Who moans for me, my darling,
   Who moans for me?

From *On the Trail of Negro Folk Songs* by Dorothy Scarborough.
Cambridge, Mass: Harvard University Press, Copyright 1925 by Harvard University Press, Copyright 1953 by Mary McDaniel Parker.

Teaching Suggestion

The circle dance directions offered here provide attention to the formal aspects of the song. Note that the dance allows sufficient time for each direction to be followed by young dancers (8 measures), an important consideration in choosing or developing dances for young children. The dance directions may be presented on large charts visible to all the participants.

Verse 1

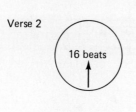

Dancers join hands, forming a circle, and walk on the beats.

Verse 2

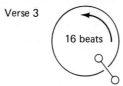

All walk to center, stepping on beats and clapping.

All walk back to original circle, stepping and clapping.

Verse 3

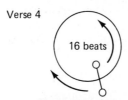

Partners join hands and walk on the beat.

Partners stay in place and walk on the beat, forming "wheels."

Verse 4

Partners stopping on the inside of the circle walk, counterclockwise, those on the outside walk clockwise. (A circle within a circle.)

All stand in place and patschen/clap.

TIDEO

Do' La Sol Mi Re Do

Skip one win - dow, Ti - de - o, Skip two win - dows, Ti - de - o

Skip three win - dows, Ti - de - o. Jin - gle at the win - dow, Ti - de - o.

Ti - de - o, Ti - de - o, Jin - gle at the win - dow, Ti - de - o.

Teacher Preparation

1. Be prepared to assist the children in their reading of the syllables *mi-sol-do'* on "Ti-de-o." Practice the hand signs for the ascending minor third and perfect fourth. High *do'* is expressed with a closed fist at arm's length overhead.

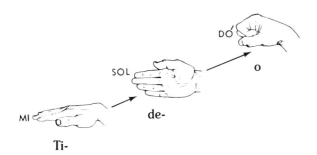

2. Prepare a color-coded accompaniment chart showing the C Major and G_7 chords. There are two strums per measure on beats 1 and 3.

Teaching Suggestions

1. Ask a student to play *mi-sol-do'* on the glockenspiel or bells when the class sings the song.

2. Ask the class which melodic syllable is sung at the end of the song and which at the beginning. Have a student locate *do* at the piano, xylophone, or pitch pipe. Assist the class in finding the beginning pitch from *do* (*do-re-mi*).

3. *Circle Dance:* The class forms a circle and joins hands high in the air to make "windows." They step in place on the beat of the song. One dancer skips in and out through the "windows," stopping to "jingle at the window" at the direction of the lyrics (use jingle clogs). At her last stopping place in the song she "jingles at the window" and hands her instrument to the nearest student and takes her place in the circle. The dance resumes with a new soloist as the song is repeated.

THE COLORADO TRAIL

Teacher Preparation

1. Practice the hand sign for the high *do'*.

sol la do'
Lyrics: All a- long

The eighth dotted quarter pattern

2. Tap out the rhythm for the syncopation in measure 6 through this preparatory exercise.

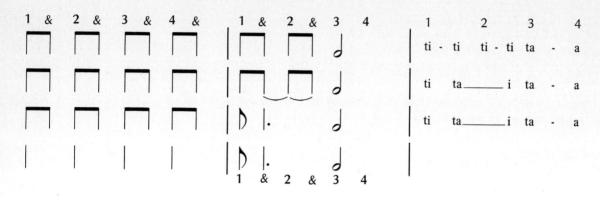

3. Locate these chords on your piano keyboard and resonator bells:

F   Major   F-A-C
B♭ Major   F-B♭-D
C₇   E-B♭-C

The chords are indicated in this song score over the first beat of each measure. Practice playing one chord per measure on the first beats.

CAPE COD GIRLS

Do' La Sol Mi Re Do Sol,

1. Cape Cod girls they have no combs, Heave a - way, heave a - way. They comb their hair with cod - fish bones, We are bound for Aus - tra - lia!

Heave a - way my bul - ly bul - ly boys, Heave a - way, heave a - way,

Heave a - way and don't you make a noise, We are bound for Aus - tra - lia.

2. Cape Cod boys they have no sleds
Heave away, heave away,
They slide down hill on codfish heads
We are bound for Australia.
Heave away my bully bully boys
Heave away, heave away,
Heave away and don't you make a noise
We are bound for Australia.

Teacher Preparation

1. The symbol 𝄵 is called *alla breve* which, translated, means *according to the breve*. In past centuries breve referred to a half note, so 𝄵 assigns a half-note to represent the beat. The meter signature for alla breve is $\frac{2}{2}$, and is often called *cut time*.

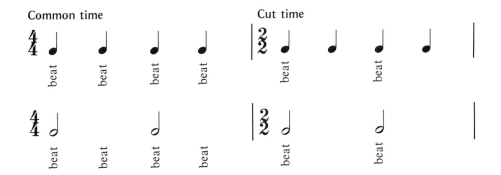

Read the lyrics of "Cape Cod Girls" aloud and sway or clap on the beats.

2. Practice singing the intervals and showing the relative pitches with the hand signs for a) "Cape Cod girls they have no combs" and b) the octave interval on "-lia" (end of measure 8) and "heave" (measure 9).

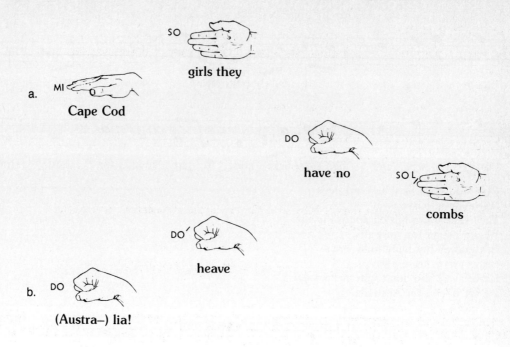

3. Prepare a guitar or autoharp accompaniment using these chords:

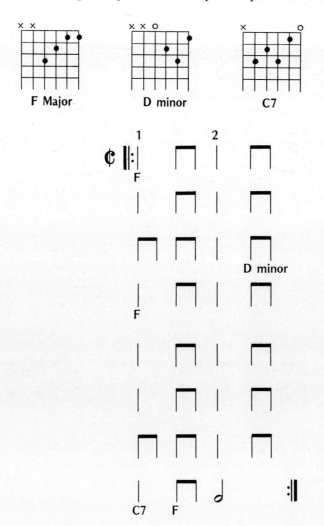

Teaching Suggestions

1. Select a soloist or small group to alternate with the class in a statement-response format.

Soloist: Cape Cod girls they have no combs,
Group: Heave away, heave away.
Soloist: They comb their hair with codfish bones,
Group: We are bound for Australia!
   All: *Chorus*

2. Assist a student in using resonator bells on "We are bound for Australia" (twice) and on the high *do'* (F) with "Heave away" in the chorus.

SOURWOOD MOUNTAIN

Kentucky Mountain Song

Do' La Sol Mi Re Do La, Sol,

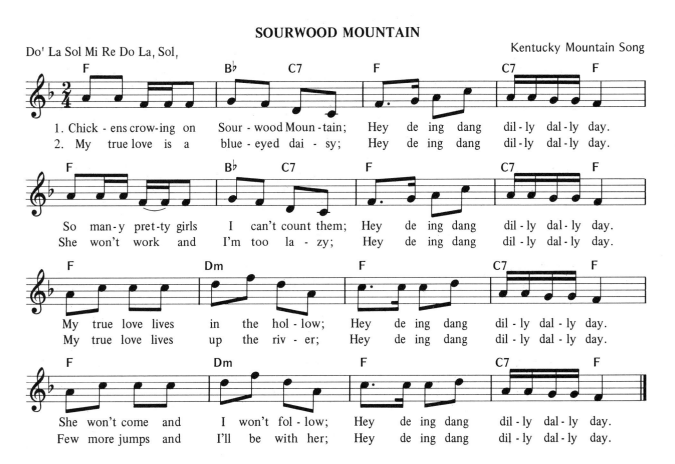

1. Chick-ens crow-ing on Sour-wood Moun-tain; Hey de ing dang dil-ly dal-ly day.
2. My true love is a blue-eyed dai-sy; Hey de ing dang dil-ly dal-ly day.

So man-y pret-ty girls I can't count them; Hey de ing dang dil-ly dal-ly day.
She won't work and I'm too la-zy; Hey de ing dang dil-ly dal-ly day.

My true love lives in the hol-low; Hey de ing dang dil-ly dal-ly day.
My true love lives up the riv-er; Hey de ing dang dil-ly dal-ly day.

She won't come and I won't fol-low; Hey de ing dang dil-ly dal-ly day.
Few more jumps and I'll be with her; Hey de ing dang dil-ly dal-ly day.

Teaching Suggestions

1. When the class has learned the song by rote and knows it well, you may use it to review some rhythmic notation and introduce the dotted eighth/sixteenth pattern.

Write on chalkboard:

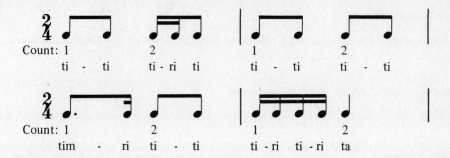

2. Assist the class in studying the form of the song. Are there phrases that are alike? Different? Do the identical phrases use the same chords in the accompaniment? Do the words, "Hey de ing dang dilly dally day," always have the same melody? The form is AABB. How is the second A slightly different from the first?

LITTLE DAVID

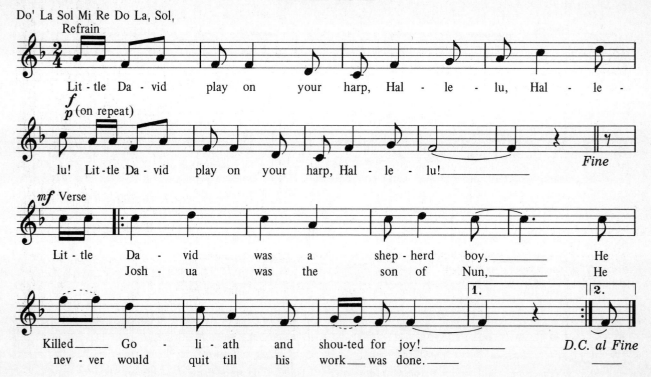

Teaching Suggestions

1. Ask a student to play an autoharp accompaniment for this song using the F Major chord and strumming on beat 1 of each measure.

2. Have your students follow you in performing this accompaniment with movement.

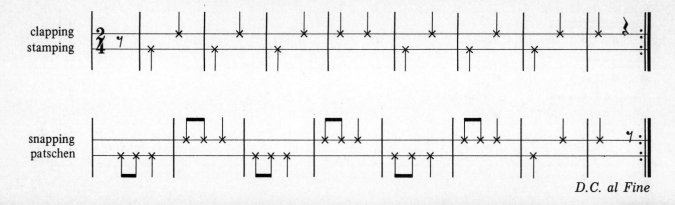

3. Ask the class for suggestions in creating a rhythm band instrumental accompaniment using drums, tambourines, wood blocks, and triangles. Have them write out their ideas for rhythm ostinatos derived from song fragments. Although suggested dynamics are shown in the score, give the children an opportunity to experiment with their own ideas.

'DESE BONES GONNA RISE AGAIN

Teaching Suggestions

1. Help the class to read the eighth and sixteenth note combinations by dividing the group into three sections. Ask Group I to read and tap the beats, while Group II reads and taps the even subdivisions of the beats and Group III taps and chants the durational syllables of the rhythm in measure 3.

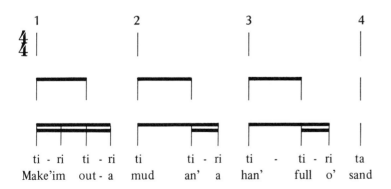

2. Select a soloist or small group for the sections marked solo, and assign the larger group to the chorus.

3. Ask a student to play resonator bells or glockenspiel with the choral response, ''Dese bones gonna rise again.''

4. Perform the following movement accompaniment four times.

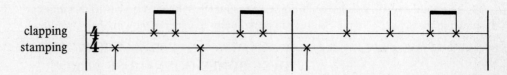

5. Accompaniment with Orff instruments:

An Orff accompaniment in C
pentatonic

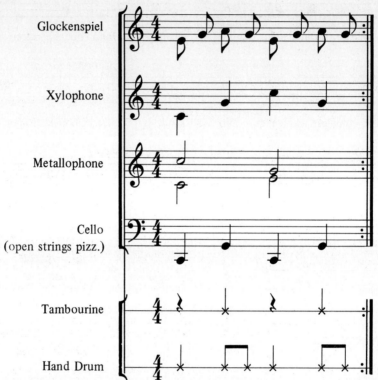

6. Introduce the hand sign for *re'*:

Take care to make sure the hand position is above *do'* at arm's length overhead.

Introducing *re'*

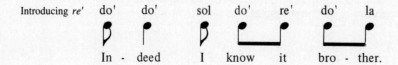

THAT GREAT GETTING UP MORNING

Mi' Do' La Sol Mi Re Do

Teacher Preparation

1. This song has a range encompassing a 10th and introduces the syllable *mi'* which   *Introducing mi'*
is indicated with a horizontal hand position at arm's length over the head. Write the notes
that appear in the song and practice singing them by syllables or numbers with hand signs.

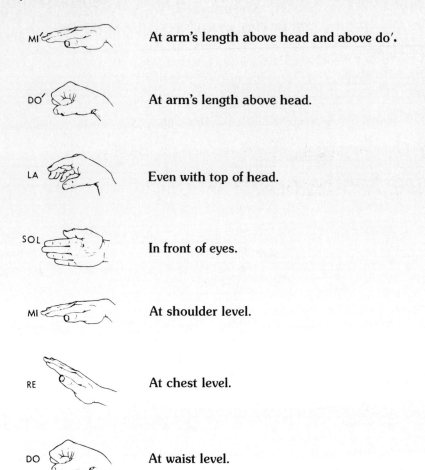

MI' — At arm's length above head and above do'.

DO' — At arm's length above head.

LA — Even with top of head.

SOL — In front of eyes.

MI — At shoulder level.

RE — At chest level.

DO — At waist level.

2. Write out a movement accompaniment which includes stamping, clapping, and snapping. Use these patterns in your scheme: ¢ 𝅗𝅥 𝅘𝅥 𝅘𝅥 and 𝅘𝅥 𝅘𝅥 𝅗𝅥. Make a change in your plan after the first 8 measures to reflect the major divisions in the song's form. Teach your accompaniment to your methods class.

Teaching Suggestion

Assist your class as they prepare their own accompaniment with Orff instruments.

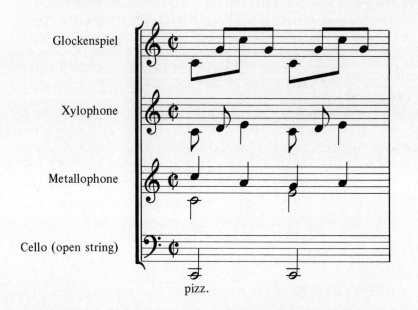

Part 4

Diatonic Songs, Piano and Recorder Practice, Harmonic Concepts

Students prepared for the more advanced curriculum are introduced to diatonic songs and the work associated with them: the concepts of whole and half steps, major and minor scales and modes, and the chords that are commonly required to accompany the new materials. The piano keyboard functions as a valuable aid in teaching and reinforcing the reading and writing skills. Two-part songs and harmonizations in thirds and sixths are added to the singing skills. Recorders enhance the Orff ensembles that accompany songs and movement activities.

New rhythms and forms are studied and applied to the performance and reading skills at this level. These include compound and irregular meters, and rondo and ABA forms.

The work in elementary creativity is extended to include the child's composition of a song's melody on a known rhythm. His or her improvisatory skills are expanded through lengthening the echo-movement exercises and through leading the other children in phrase-building patterns.

Opportunities for children to arrange songs with instrumental accompaniments and stories with sound effects are appropriate for this age group. Public performances for holidays or parents' meetings should include children's works and be an outgrowth of the variety of activities found at each class meeting. In this way schools can provide communities with an awareness of the scope of general classroom music and its impact on the childrens' aesthetic development.

LOVE SOMEBODY

Sol Fa Mi Re Do

1. Love some-bod-y, yes I do, Love some-bod-y, yes I do,

Love some-bod-y, yes I do, Love some-bod-y but I won't tell who.

2. Love somebody, can't guess who!
   Love somebody, can't guess who!
   Love somebody, can't guess who!
   Love somebody, but I won't tell who.

Teacher Preparation

1. Practice the hand sign for the syllable *fa,* which is introduced in this song.

Fa and its hand sign

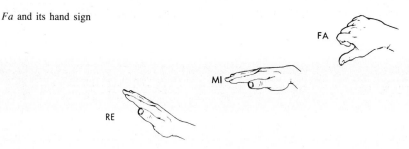

2. A *chord* may be defined as any combination of 3 or more tones sounded simultaneously, and can be built on any step of a scale. Roman numerals are used to identify chords according to the scale step numbers of their roots. The C major chord is identified as the **I** chord in the key of C major because its *root* is C, the first step of the scale. Similarly the G chord is identified as the **V** chord in C Major because its root is G, the fifth tone of the scale. The V_7 is created when a fourth tone is sounded with the G major triad making an interval of a seventh between the root and the fourth tone. (Count the distance from G up to F.) A chord with this added tone is called a *seventh chord.* Chords may be played in root position, or may be *inverted,* with the notes rearranged. The chords shown below appear more frequently than others in children's music.

Primary chords

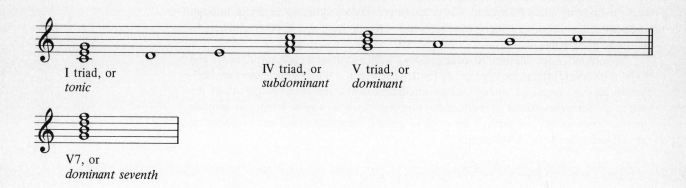

I triad, or
tonic

IV triad, or
subdominant

V triad, or
dominant

V7, or
dominant seventh

As you perform accompaniments with these *primary* chords you will hear that the tonic functions as a "home base" with the harmony moving toward and away from it. Locate these chords on the piano: C Major and G_7. These are the **I** and $\mathbf{V_7}$ chords in C Major.

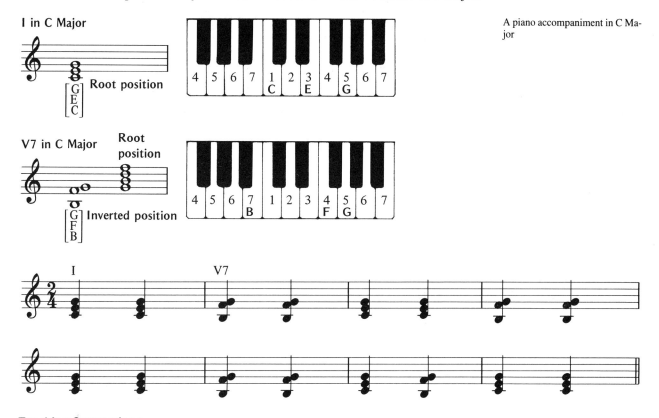

A piano accompaniment in C Major

Teaching Suggestions

1. Use this simple song to review the durational syllables. Ask the class to read:

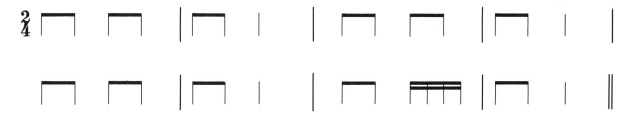

2. Ask the class to identify like and unlike measures. Ask how measure 4 differs from measure 8. Have them exchange measures 4 and 8, and sing the song ending on *re*. Ask them which note and syllable sounds "correct" to complete the song.

3. Divide the class into two groups. Ask each group to sing alternate measures with syllables and hand signs, or with numbers and note names.

		Scale numbers
Group I:	do mi sol sol	(1 3 5 5)
Group II:	re mi fa	(2 3 4)
Group I:	do mi sol sol	(1 3 5 5)
Group II:	re mi re	(2 3 2)
Group I:	do mi sol sol	(1 3 5 5)
Group II:	re mi fa	(2 3 4)
Group I:	mi mi re re re re	(33 22 22)
Group II:	do mi do	(1 3 1)

4. Write the C Major scale for the class. Explain that chords are built from scale tones. Chord **I** is built on the first tone of the scale. Chord **V** is built on the fifth tone of the scale with the fourth tone of the scale sometimes added to it to create the **V₇.**

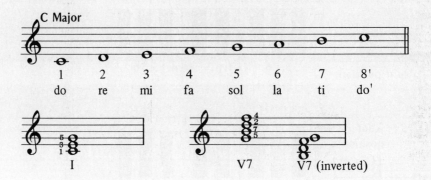

5. Ask the class to select one of the chords for each measure by relating the notes in the melody to the notes in the chords. Which chord contains the notes found in measure 1? Measure 2? etc.

RECORDER PRACTICE: Playing B, A, G

1. Locate these notes on your recorder, using the correct fingerings. Remember to use your left hand for these notes.

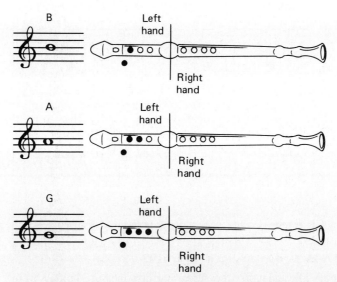

2. Tune your instrument with the piano or pitch pipe. If the pitch is too low, push in the head joint. If it is too high, pull it out. Blow gently when you play and articulate the notes with "doo" (never "hoo"). Cover the holes completely and keep your other fingers near the tone holes while you are playing.

3. Follow this format for your beginning lessons: Listen as your instructor plays a measure. Then echo his or her playing.

THE DEAF WOMAN'S COURTSHIP

Sol Fa Mi Re Do

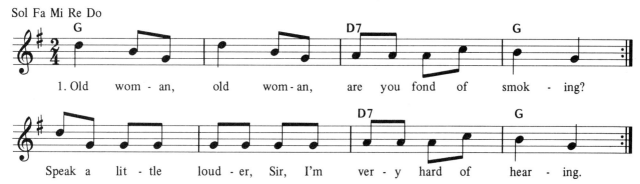

1. Old wom-an, old wom-an, are you fond of smok-ing?
Speak a lit-tle loud-er, Sir, I'm ver-y hard of hear-ing.

2. Old woman, old woman, are you fond of carding?
   Speak a little louder, Sir, I'm rather hard of hearing.

3. Old woman, old woman, don't you want me to court you?
   Speak a little louder, Sir, I just began to hear you.

4. Old woman, old woman, don't you want to marry me?
   Lord have mercy on my soul, I think that now I hear you.

Teaching Suggestions

1. Show the class a piano keyboard, preferably a large chart easily seen by all members of the group. Assist them in finding ascending or descending whole or half steps from any given key. These may be indicated as follows:

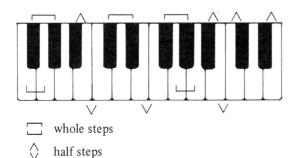

☐ whole steps

◇ half steps

2. Help the class locate the notes of the G Major scale by locating the whole and half steps required for a major scale. Ask them which step of the scale will be a black note on the keyboard in G Major.

Any Major Scale: 1   2   3   4   5   6   7   8

G Major Scale: G   A   B   C   D   E   F♯   G

The major scale:
whole steps, half steps

3. Write chords **I** and **V₇** for the class. Explain that these are also called G Major and D₇ in the key of G Major because their chord roots are G and D.

4. Assist the class in preparing an accompaniment for the song by relating the notes in each measure to the notes of the chords. Demonstrate that in a two-chord accompaniment the **I** chord will dominate. Changes to **V₇** occur when the melodic notes are derived from the notes in the **V₇** chord.

WHEN THE SAINTS GO MARCHING IN

Teaching Suggestions

1. After the children have learned the song well, help them sing it with "Swing Low Sweet Chariot" as a partner song. Have each group sing both songs.

A. Oh when the saints-----Go marching in------O when the
B.   Swing low--- sweet---- chariot

2. Work with the class to accompany the song with body motions.

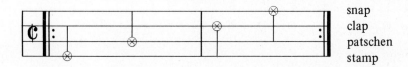

snap
clap
patschen
stamp

3. Rhythm instrument accompaniment:

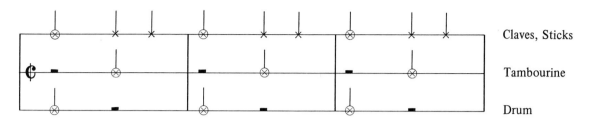

Claves, Sticks

Tambourine

Drum

OATS AND BEANS AND BARLEY

Sol Fa Mi Re Do

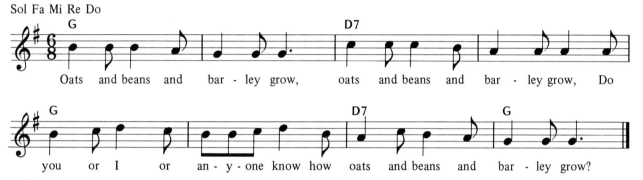

Oats and beans and bar - ley grow, oats and beans and bar - ley grow, Do

you or I or an - y - one know how oats and beans and bar - ley grow?

2. First the farmer sows his seed
Then he stands and takes his ease
Stamps his foot and claps his hands
And turns around to view the land.

3. Waiting for a partner
Waiting for a partner
Break the ring and choose one in
While all the others dance and sing.

Teaching Suggestions

1. To assist the students in learning to read the compound meter $\frac{6}{8}$, ask them to clap with you:

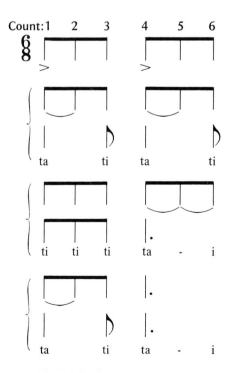

2. Use a color-coded accompaniment chart to indicate chord changes to use with Orff instruments.

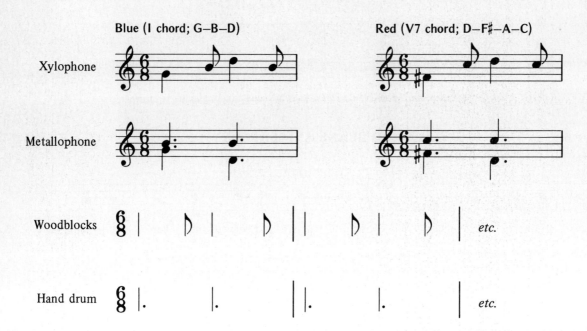

3. This recorder exercise on B-A-G has the same rhythm as "Oats and Beans." Ask your students to play it with you and then have a group perform it as a second part with singers.

Recorder

WRITING PRACTICE

1. Write in the notes for the syllables and scale numbers that are given.

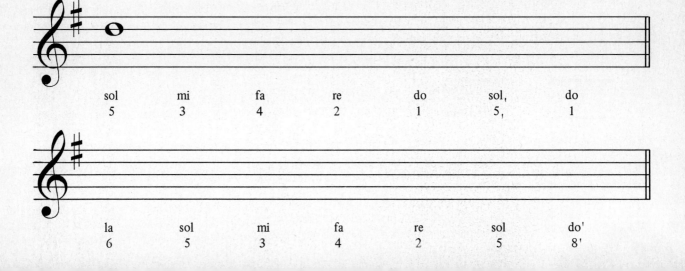

2. Write the chords that are indicated.

3. Write in the rhythmic notation to make each measure complete.

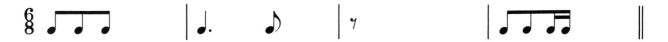

4. Identify each ascending interval as a whole or half step.

G-A	B♭-C
B-C	E-F
F♯-G	C♯-D
D-E	E-F♯
A-B♭	E♭-F

Skill-Building in Musical Improvisation and Elementary Composition

Children's success in musical improvisation and elementary composition is dependent upon a well-developed sense of rhythmic security, an awareness of melodic contour, and a feeling for phrase and form. Continued work with echo-movement and phrase building activities enables the teacher to increase her students' self confidence when they approach creative experiences that employ these music "basics." The chanting of verses and rhymes in the various meters provides review and opportunities for introduction of new rhythm patterns. Children in the upper grades are able to complete teacher-initiated verses and jingles. The transfer of rhythms from speech patterns to instruments allows for melodic improvisation with mallet instruments. Finally, melodic composition can seem much less overwhelming if the children are permitted to begin with a known element—the rhythm of a verse. The methods class should develop ways to use the $\frac{6}{8}$ verses included in this section that will assist children in their creative activities while increasing their reading readiness.

Rock-a-bye, baby, the cradle is green;
Father's a nobleman, mother's a queen; and
Betty's a lady, and wears a gold ring; and
Johnny's a drummer and drums for the king.

Pussy-cat, pussy-cat where have you been?
I've been to London to visit the Queen!
Pussy-cat, pussy-cat, what did you there? I
Frightened a little mouse under her chair.

Hey! diddle, diddle the cat and the fiddle the
Cow jumped over the moon. The
Little dog laughed to see such sport, and the
Dish ran away with the spoon.

Little Miss Muffet, sat on a tuffet,
Eating her curds and whey! There
Came a great spider and sat down beside her and
Frightened Miss Muffet away.

Verses in $\frac{6}{8}$ to chant and play

Little Jack Horner, sat in a corner,
Eating a Christmas pie. He
Put in his thumb and pulled out a plum and said,
"What a good boy am I."

Intery, mintery, cutery corn,
Apple seed and apple thorn.
Wine, briar, lumber lock,
Three geese in a flock.
One flew east, one flew west, and
One flew over the goose's nest.

Jack, be nimble, Jack be quick,
Jack jump over the candlestick.
Jump it lively, jump it quick, but
Don't knock over the candlestick.
Jack be nimble, Jack be quick,
Jack jump over the candlestick.

Hippety hop to the barber shop, to
Get a stick of candy.
One for you and one for me, and
One for Sister Mandy.

Hickory, dickory, sackory down!
How many miles to Richmond town?
Turn to the left and turn to the right, and
You may get there by Saturday night!

Teaching Suggestions

1. Assist the children as they perform the verses with dynamic and tempo contrasts.
2. Divide the class into groups and have them chant 2 or more verses simultaneously.
3. Ask the children to create ostinato patterns derived from the rhythms of the verses to perform on rhythm instruments of their choice while chanting.

4. Assist the children as they develop movement accompaniments for the chanting.

5. Help the class create an introduction and coda for a chant. These should be in the meter of the verse and may be performed on instruments, with movements, or a combination of techniques.

Verse   Jack be nimble, Jack be quick...

6. Show the class how to chant in 2 and 3 part canons.

To create a 3 part canon divide the class into 3 groups. Each group chants the entire verse. Group 2 enters after group 1 has completed one line, and group 3 enters after group 2 has completed one line.

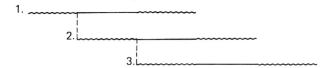

7. Have the class perform the rhythms of several verses simultaneously on rhythm instruments.

arranged by R. Herrold

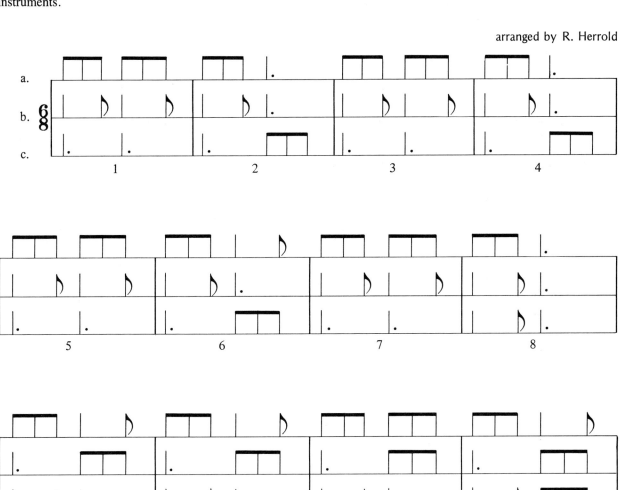

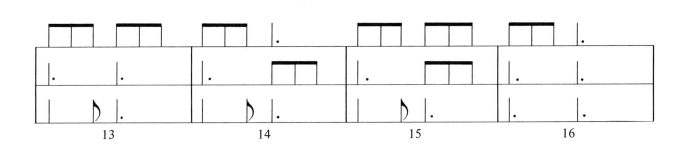

a. measures 1—8   Rock-a-bye, baby, thy cradle is green;
                          Father's a nobleman, mother's a queen; and
                          Betty's a lady, and wears a gold ring; and
                          Johnny's a drummer and drums for the king.

a. measures 9—16   Ride a cock-horse to Banbury Cross, to
                          See a fine lady upon a white horse, with
                          Rings on her fingers and bells on her toes,
                          She shall have music wherever she goes.

Teaching Suggestion

Using the Rhythm Exercise Based on Verses in ⁶⁄₈

1. Divide the class into three groups and have them tap out a, b, and c simultaneously. Then switch parts, until each student has experienced the rhythm of each part.

2. Assign rhythm instruments to each part. Sandpaper blocks for part a, wood blocks for part b, and hand drums for part c are one possible instrumentation.

3. Have the students create their own movement schemes for the three parts, using stamping, patschen, clapping, finger snapping.

COMPLETING A COMPOSITION IN $\frac{6}{8}$

Teaching Suggestion

Ask the students to complete this song by using the syllables *la, sol, fa, mi, re* and *do*. Their placement on the staff is shown below. Assist them with the rhythm of the four incomplete measures by having them chant and then clap the verse. Write the verse on the board and ask the class to indicate where the accented words are. Help them to see that the first note in a measure corresponds to an accented word or syllable.

la   sol   fa   mi   re   do

THE BEAR WENT OVER THE MOUNTAIN

La Sol Fa Mi Re Do

The bear went o-ver the moun-tain. The bear went o-ver the moun-tain. The

bear went o-ver the moun-tain, To see what he could see._____ And

all that he could see_____ And all that he could see Was the

oth - er side of the moun - tain, The oth - er side of the moun - tain, The

oth - er side of the moun - tain Was all that he could see._____

Teaching Suggestions

1. Ask the class to practice the rhythm for the song in an echo clapping exercise in groups of 6 beats. Have them tap their feet in 2 throughout the patterns.

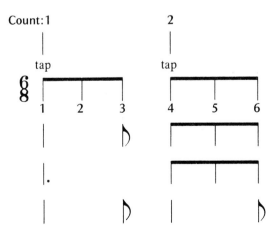

teacher claps, students echo patterns

2. Show the class that the upbeat is understood as beat 6 of an incomplete measure.

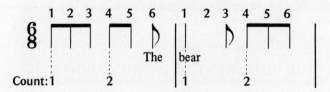

3. Assist the students in writing the **IV** (C Major) chord in the key of G Major.

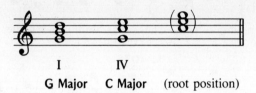

I   IV

G Major   C Major   (root position)

A Piano Accompaniment in G Major: I, IV, and V7 chords

The bear went over the moun - tain, The bear went over the moun - tain the

bear went over the moun - tain to see what he could see.   And

all that he could see;   And all that he could see, Was the

other side of the moun - tain, the other side of the moun - tain the

other side of the moun - tain, was all that he could see.____

RECORDER PRACTICE: Playing C, B, A, G

1. Add C to your recorder fingerings.

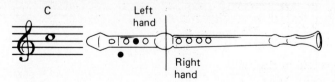

Left hand

Right hand

2. Use an echo style practice session with your instructor to warm up. Then write out an exercise on C, B, A, G and teach it using echo style.

3. Use these pieces in planning a lesson to teach to your methods class or a group of children.

from "The Bear Went Over the Mountain"

Marching

HE'S GOT THE WHOLE WORLD IN HIS HANDS

La Sol Fa Mi Re Do

2. He's got the wind and the rain in His hands.

3. He's got that little tiny baby in His hands.

4. He's got you and me, brother, in His hands.

5. He's got everybody in His hands.

6. He's got the whole world in His hands.

Teacher Preparation

1. Practice performing a simple two chord accompaniment on guitar or autoharp strumming on beats 1 and 3 of each measure. Teach the song by rote to your methods class or a group of children.

2. Write out an accompaniment chart for children using these rhythms:

3. Develop a plan to give variety to the presentation of the 6 verses.

OH SUSANNAH

La Sol Fa Mi Re Do

Stephen Foster

I___ come from Al - a - ba - ma with my ban - jo on my knee, I'm
going to Lou' - si - an - a my_____ true love for to see.

Refrain

Oh, Su - san - na, Oh, don't you cry for me, For I
come from Al - a - ba - ma with my ban - jo on my knee.

Teacher Preparation

1. Write the F Major scale and put in the key signature.

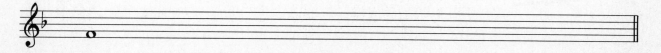

2. Write the chords indicated below the staff.

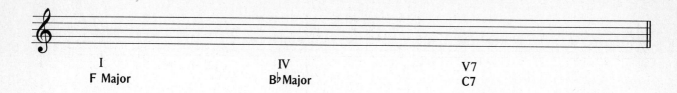

I	IV	V7
F Major	B♭ Major	C7

Teaching Suggestions

1. The melodic syllable *fa* is isolated in this song at the beginning of the refrain. The ascending interval F-B♭ on "see. Oh" is a perfect fourth, two whole steps and one half step. Children may recall this interval from the opening of "The Wedding March."

Ask the class to sing *do-fa-la,* following your hand signs.

Hand signs: practice using *fa*

2. Explain that the upbeat is the last half of beat 2 in an incomplete measure.

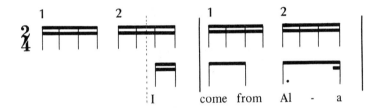

3. Durational syllable practice:

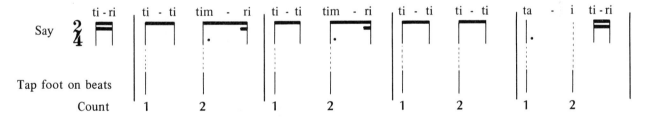

ALABAMA GAL

La Sol Fa Mi Re Do

Al - a - ba - ma gal won't you come out to - night,

come out to - night, come out to - night. Al - a - ba - ma gal won't you

come out to - night and dance by the light of the moon.

Teacher Preparation

Review and practice the hand signs for these patterns:

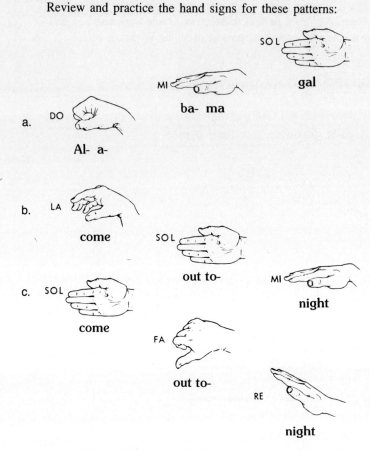

Teaching Suggestions

1. Ask the students to find the measures that are the same as a) and b), and the measure that most clearly resembles c). Have them follow your hand signs as you assist them in singing the syllables for these measures. Then ask them to read the melodic syllables from the chalkboard or overhead projector.

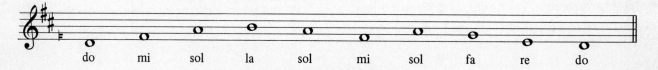

do   mi   sol   la   sol   mi   sol   fa   re   do

2. Lead the class in this echo-movement exercise to prepare them for the characteristic rhythm of the song:

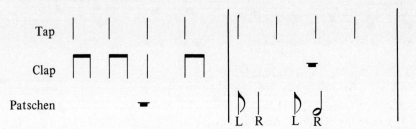

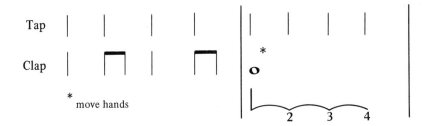

3. Durational syllables practice:

4. Ask the students for their ideas for developing a rhythm instrument accompaniment. Here are some patterns that have been suggested by children:

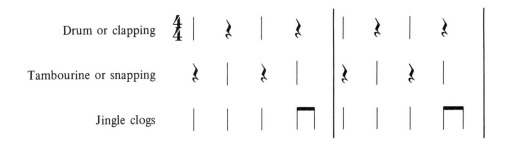

MICHAEL ROW THE BOAT ASHORE

2. Sister, help to trim the sail, Hallelujah!
   Sister, help to trim the sail, Hallelujah!

3. River's deep and the river is wide, Hallelujah!
   Milk and honey on the other side, Hallelujah!

4. Jordan's river is chilly and cold, Hallelujah!
   Chills the body but not the soul, Hallelujah!

Teacher Preparation

Practice a guitar or autoharp accompaniment, strumming on an even eighth note pattern throughout.

Guitar Chords

D Major   G Major   E minor   A7

Teaching Suggestion

Ask the children for their ideas for creating a different accompaniment and mood for each verse. Use resonator bells, rhythm instruments, contrasting dynamics, and soloist-group changes.

Use glockenspiels or resonator bells on measures 3–4 and 7–8.

BY'N BYE

*glockenspiel or bells

RECORDER PRACTICE: Playing C, B, A, G, F, E

1. Locate F and E with your right hand. Keep the left hand fingers in place as indicated.

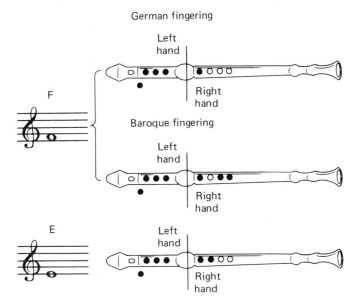

2. Warm up on F and E by echoing your instructor's playing.

3. Now practice this four-tone piece.

4. Use the six tones to which you've been introduced.

2nd part for BY'N BYE

RING, RING DE BANJO

by Stephen Foster

Do' La Sol Fa Mi Re Do

* ₵ alla breve

Teacher Preparation

1. Study and practice the hand signs for the section of this song that includes the high *do'*.

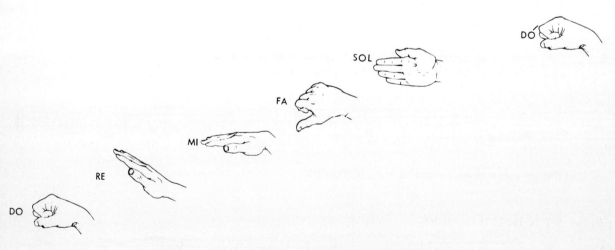

2. Review the C Major scale and locate the **I** and **V₇** chords on the piano. Then study the bass clef (known as the F clef because it indicates the position of F on the staff). Find the notes on the piano that correspond to the notation.

The bass clef

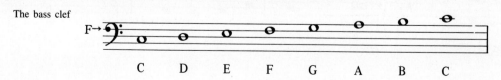

F→

C   D   E   F   G   A   B   C

3. Practice this piano accompaniment for "Ring, Ring de Banjo." Note that the left hand part, indicated by the bass clef, makes use of only two notes, the roots of the two chords.

Teaching Suggestions

Children can play their own accompaniment for this traditional favorite. Ask them to select the resonator bells needed to play the **I** and **V₇** chords in C Major.

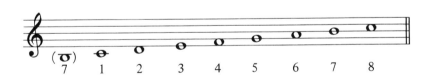 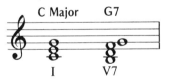

Autoharps may be added to the bell accompaniment for the refrain section to provide contrast with the verse. Have the class experiment with dynamic changes, too.

Select three players for the C Major chord; four players for the G₇ chord.

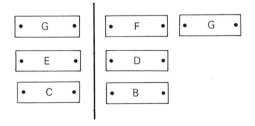

READING AND IMPROVISATION PRACTICE: Rondo

Create a rhythmic *rondo* with your class. The A group will perform the returning pattern after each contrasting pattern. Soloists in the class should improvise the B, C, and D sections. The rondo may be clapped, stepped, or performed on instruments.

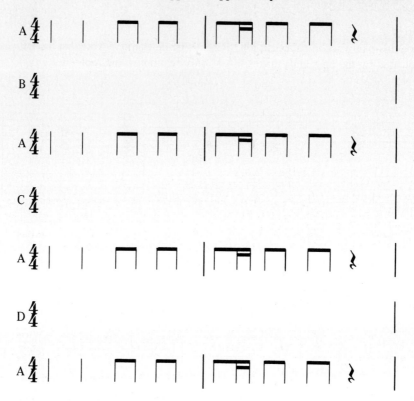

SANTY MALONEY

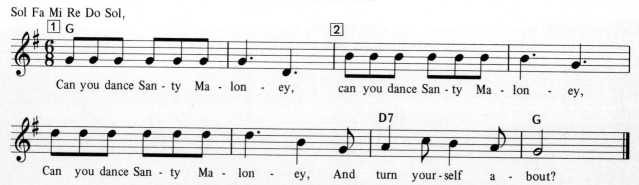

Sol Fa Mi Re Do Sol,

Can you dance San - ty Ma - lon - ey, can you dance San - ty Ma - lon - ey,

Can you dance San - ty Ma - lon - ey, And turn your-self a - bout?

Teaching Suggestions

1. Have the class sing the song as a strict canon, or *round*. Explain to the children that a round is a composition in which one melody is sung or played by different people or instruments at different times. Although many rounds are harmonized by one chord, the tonic, this one has two chords. Measures 5 and 7, when sung together, are compatible because the note D in measure 5 is also found in the D₇ chord of measure 7.

2. Ask the class to create name substitutions for Santy Maloney and action substitutions for "turn yourself about".

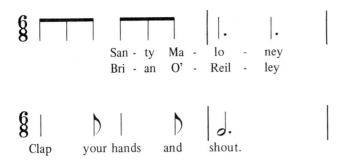

San - ty Ma - lo - ney
Bri - an O' - Reil - ley

Clap   your hands   and   shout.

FOUR IN A BOAT

Sol Fa Mi Re Do La, Sol,

Four in a boat and the tide rolls high,   Four in a boat and the tide rolls high;

Four in a boat and the tide rolls high,   Get you a pret-ty one bye and bye.

Teaching Suggestions

1. Give the children a review session in reading syllables or numbers.

do	mi	do	la,	sol,	do	mi	sol	re	sol	do	fa	mi	re	do
1	3	1	6,	5,	1	3	5	2	5	1	4	3	2	1

2. Ask the class if the melodic contour is the same each time "tide rolls high" is sung. Ask them to select bells that correspond to the notes in the three patterns for these lyrics.

3. Assist the class in adding a harmonization to the melody on the last line of the song. Have them write with you, showing them that each note is a third above the melody.

Get   you   a   pret - ty   one   bye   and   bye.

FATHER GRUMBLE

2. "But you must milk the tiny cow
For fear she should go dry
And you must feed the little pigs
That are within the sty,
And you must watch the bracket hen
Lest she should lay astray,
And you must wind the reel of yarn
That I spun yesterday."

3. The old woman took the staff in her hand
And went to drive the plough;
The old man took the pail in his hand
And went to milk the cow;
But Tiny hinched and Tiny flinched
And Tiny cocked her nose
And Tiny hit the old man such a kick
That the blood ran down to his toes.

4. 'T'was, "Hey my good cow," and "How, my good cow,"
And "Now my good cow, stand still.
If ever I milk this cow again,
'Twill be against my will."
And when he'd milked the tiny cow
For fear she should go dry,
Why, then he fed the little pigs
That were within the sty.

5. And then he watched the bracket hen,
Lest she should lay astray,
But he forgot the reel of yarn
His wife spun yesterday.
He swore by all the leaves on the tree,
And all the stars in heaven,
That his wife could do more work in a day
Than he could do in seven.

Taken from Eloise Linscott's "Songs of North America."
Used by permission of the Shoestring Press, Inc.

Teacher Preparation

Practice this piano accompaniment for the song. Locate the **I** and **V₇** chords. Find G and
D below middle C.

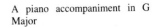

A piano accompaniment in G
Major

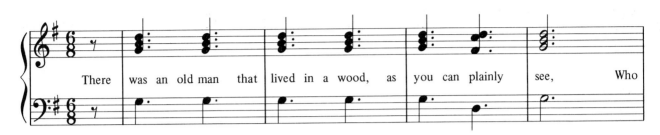

There was an old man that lived in a wood, as you can plainly see, Who

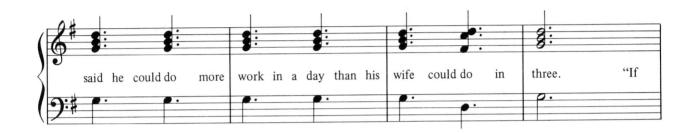

said he could do more work in a day than his wife could do in three. "If

that be so the old woman said, why this you must al - low That

you shall do my work for a day while I go drive the plough.——

Teaching Suggestions

1. Ask the class for suggested sounds that might be associated with the various animals, objects, and actions depicted in the lyrics. They might enjoy trying suggestions other classes have performed too.

Tiny cow:	glockenspiel on E and D	Using instruments
Little pigs:	bells on G,D,E,D	for sound effects
Bracket hen:	woodblocks	
Wind the reel of yarn:	sandpaper blocks (in continuous circular motion)	
Heaven:	D₇ strum on autoharp	

2. Use a different bodily movement accompaniment for each verse.

1. Sway and patschen on beat 1 of each measure.

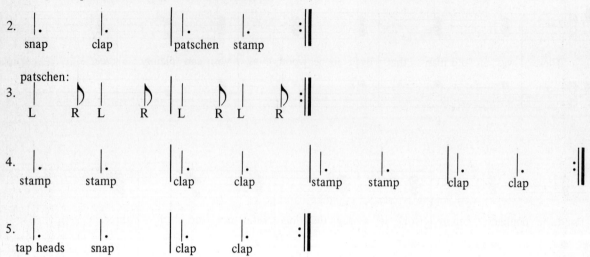

2.   snap   clap   patschen   stamp

patschen:

3.   L   R   L   R   L   R   L   R

4.   stamp   stamp   clap   clap   stamp   stamp   clap   clap

5.   tap heads   snap   clap   clap

LITTLE JOE THE WRANGLER

La Sol Fa Mi Re Do La,

1. Oh___ Lit - tle Joe, the wran-gler, he'll___ wran-gle nev - er-more; His___

days with the re - mu-da they are o'er;___ 'Twas a year a - go last A - pril that he

rode in - to our camp, Just a lit - tle Tex - as stray and all a -

lone.___ It was late___ in the eve - ning when he rode up to our camp, On a

lit - tle Tex - as po - ny he called "Chaw."___ With his bro-gan shoes and o - ver - alls, a

tough - er look - in' kid, You___ nev - er in your life be - fore had saw.___

2. He said, if we would give him work, he'd do the best he could,
   Though he didn't know straight up about a cow;
   So the boss he cut him out a mount, and kindly put him on,
   For he sorta liked this little kid somehow.
   Learned him to wrangle horses and try to know them well,
   And get them in at daylight if he could;
   To follow the chuckwagon and always hitch the team,
   And to help the wagon cook to rustle wood.

3. We had driven to the Pecos, the weather being fine;
   We had camped on the southside in a bend;
   When a norther came a-blowin', we had doubled up our guard,
   For it had taken all of us to hold them in.
   Little Joe, the wrangler, was called out with the rest;
   Though the kid had scarcely reached the herd,
   When the cattle they stampeded, like a hailstorm long they fled;
   When we were all a-ridin' for the lead.

4. Amidst the streaks of lightnin', a horse we could see in the lead,
   'Twas little Joe, the wrangler, in the lead;
   He was ridin' Ole Blue Rocket with a slicker o'er his head,
   And a-tryin' to check the cattle in their speed.
   At last we got them millin' and kind-a quieted down,
   And the extra guard back to the wagon went,
   But there was one a-missin', and we knew it at a glance;
   'Twas our little Texas stray, poor wrangling Joe.

Teacher Preparation

Write out the D Major scale and put in the key signature.

Write the chords indicated below the staff. Play them on a piano.

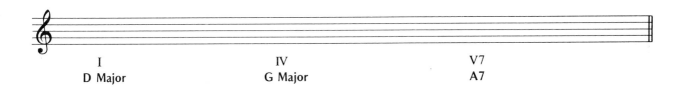

| I | IV | V7 |
| D Major | G Major | A7 |

Teaching Suggestions

1. Ask children to strum their autoharps on the beats and to create rhythm parts for temple blocks and a cow bell.

2. Use resonator bells on the chord tones appropriate for the sustained words. Assist the children in locating the bells for D Major and A_7.

measures 4 and 12

measures 8 and 16

LOOBY LOO

La Sol Fa Mi Re Do Sol,
Chorus

Arranged by R. Herrold

2. Here we go looby loo
   Here we go looby light
   Here we go looby loo
   All on a Saturday night.
   You put your right hand in
   You put your right hand out
   You shake it a little, a little, a little
   And turn yourself about.

4. Here we go looby loo
   Here we go looby light
   Here we go looby loo
   All on a Saturday night
   You put your right leg in
   You put your right leg out
   You shake it a little, a little, a little
   And turn yourself about.

3. Here we go looby loo
   Here we go looby light
   Here we go looby loo
   All on a Saturday night.
   You put your left leg in
   You put your left leg out
   You shake it a little, a little, a little
   And turn yourself about.

5. Here we go looby loo
   Here we go looby light
   Here we go looby loo
   All on a Saturday night
   You put your whole self in,
   You put your whole self out,
   You shake it a little, a little, a little
   And turn yourself about.

Teaching Suggestions

1. A circle dance created for "Looby Loo" reinforces the major divisions in the 16 measures of the song. The children form two circles, one within the other, and move in opposite directions on the beats of the chorus. Group 1 sings the soprano part, group 2 the alto part. At the verse, both groups are stationary and face the center of the circle. Their movements are directed by the different lyrics for each verse as they sing in unison.

2. The 2 part chorus may be expressed in 2 part movement while the children hum or sing softly on "loo." Have them show the question-answer style through clapping-snapping or clapping-patschen.

THE OLD CHISHOLM TRAIL

La Sol Fa Mi Re Do La, Sol,

2. I'm up in the mornin' before daylight,
   And before I sleep the moon shines bright.
   Chorus

3. Oh, it's bacon and beans 'most every day,
   I'd as soon be a-eatin' prairie hay.
   Chorus

Teaching Suggestions

1. Ask the class to follow your hand signs for these intervals derived from "The Old Chisholm Trail."

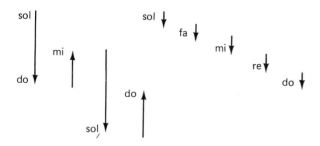

Give the class some preparatory reading practice with syllables or numbers.

sol	do	mi	sol,	do	sol	fa	mi	re	do
5	1	3	5,	1	5	4	3	2	1

2. Assist the class in harmonization by having them sing the G, C, and D₇ chords. Divide the class into two groups, one to sing the song and another to harmonize with syllables, numbers, or note names.

Vocal harmonizing on I, IV, V₇ chords

	G Major	C	D₇	G Major
	I	**IV**	**V₇**	**I**
High voices:	sol 5	la 6	sol 5	sol 5
Middle voices:	mi 3	fa 4	fa 4	mi 3
Low voices:	do 1	do 1	ti, 7	do 1

G Major	C Major	D7	G Major
I	**IV**	**V7**	**I**

3. Use a rhythm instrument accompaniment as the children sing and harmonize.

Temple blocks $\frac{4}{4}$ | . ♪ | | | . ♪ | | *etc.*

Cowbell | ⸓ ⸓ | | ⸓ ⸓ | *etc.*

RECORDER PRACTICE: The C Major Scale

1. Locate D and C on your instrument.

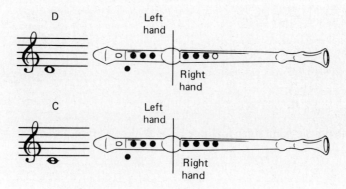

2. Listen as your instructor plays exercises first on D, then C, and, finally, combinations of the two.

3. Play the C Major scale and a piece which uses all 8 tones of the scale.

SOWING ON THE MOUNTAIN

La Sol Fa Mi Re Do La, Sol,

Sow-ing on the moun - tain   rea-ping in the val   ley;

____ Sow-ing on the moun - tain ____ rea-ping in the val   ley; ____

____ Sow-ing on the moun - tain ____ rea-ping in the val   ley; ____

____ You're gon - na   reap ____   Just what you   sow.

Teacher Preparation

A piano accompaniment in D Major

Practice this piano accompaniment in the key of D Major.

Teaching Suggestions

1. Divide the class into two groups, and ask one group to echo the other in singing the song.

3 times:

> Sowing on the mountain,
> Reaping in the valley,
> You're gonna reap
> Just what you sow.

> Sowing on the moun-tain
> Reaping in the val-ley,
> You're gonna reap
> Just what you sow

2. Ask the class for suggestions in creating a movement accompaniment. They might want to try:

a. patschen—snap—patschen—snap, *etc.*
b. stamp—clap—stamp—clap, *etc.*
c. tap foot—patschen—tap foot—clap, *etc.*

WHO BUILT THE ARK?

2. He built it long, both wide and tall,
   Plenty of room for the big and the small.
   Chorus

3. He found him an ax and a hammer too,
   He began to cut and began to hew.
   Chorus

4. And every time that hammer ring,
   Old Noah shout and Noah sing.
   Chorus

5. Now in come the animals two by two,
   Hippopotamus and kangaroo.
   Chorus

6. Now in come the animals three by three,
   Two big cats and a bumblebee.
   Chorus

7. Now in come the animals four by four,
   Two through the windows and two through the door.
   Chorus

Teaching Suggestions

1. Add a second vocal part in thirds and sixths to the chorus the second time through.

2. Use a question and answer style in singing the song. The questions may be sung by a soloist or small group.

3. Vary the dynamics. Sing the two-part chorus *pianissimo, pp*. Change dynamic levels for the verses.

4. Ask the class for ideas for creating sound effects on key words in the lyrics such as ''big,'' ''small,'' ''ax,'' ''hammer,'' ''ring,'' ''hippopotamus,'' ''bumblebee.''

GOODBYE, MY JANIE

Sol Fa Mi Re Do Ti,

2. My heart will evermore be true,
   Goodbye my Janie, goodbye;
   Though now we sadly say adieu,
   Goodbye, my Janie, goodbye.

Teaching Suggestions

1. Assist the class in following your hand signs as they sing these syllables.

*Ti*₁ below *do* and its hand sign

2. Write the corresponding notation for the hand signs shown above, and ask the class to sing the syllables or scale numbers with you.

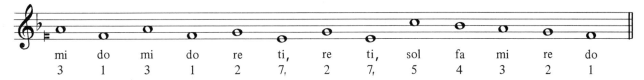

| mi | do | mi | do | re | ti₁ | re | ti₁ | sol | fa | mi | re | do |
| 3 | 1 | 3 | 1 | 2 | 7₁ | 2 | 7₁ | 5 | 4 | 3 | 2 | 1 |

3. Select some class members to sing this second part on the refrain.

By - low, my ba - by, by - low, my ba - by,

by - low, my ba - by good - bye my Ja - nie, good - bye._____

4. Use resonator bells or glockenspiel on the repeated melody of the refrain:

"By-low, my baby"
A F B♭ A F

RECORDER PRACTICE: F♯ and B♭

1. Locate F♯ and B♭ on your instrument. These new tones will permit you to play in G Major, E minor, F Major, and D minor.

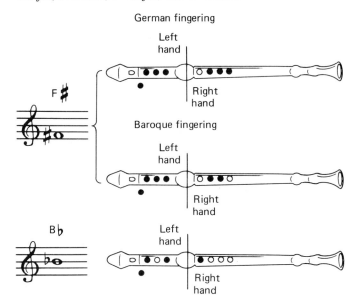

2. Echo your instructor after each measure.

3. Practice each piece by yourself. Then play with the class.

SHOO FLY SHOO

Sol Fa Mi Re Do Ti,

1. Fly in the but-ter-milk, shoo fly shoo!   Fly in the but-ter-milk, shoo fly shoo!

Fly in the but-ter-milk, shoo fly shoo!   Skip to my Lou, my dar - ling.

Lou, Lou, skip to my Lou. Lou, Lou, skip to my Lou.

Lou, Lou, skip to my Lou. Skip to my Lou, my dar - ling.

2. Little red wagon painted blue, *etc.*

3. Cat's in the buttermilk, what'll we do? *etc.*

4. Lost my partner, What'll I do? *etc.*

5. I'll get another one, prettier than you! , *etc.*

6. Can't get a red bird, a blue bird will do. *etc.*

Teacher Preparation

Practice this piano accompaniment for "Shoo Fly Shoo."

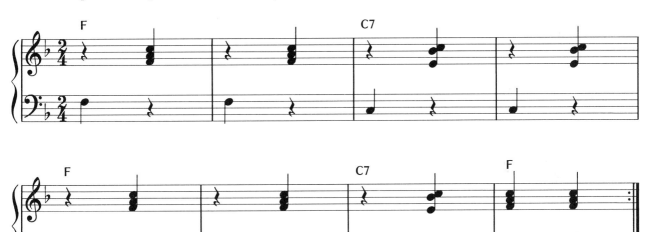

Teaching Suggestions

   1. Have students provide their own accompaniment with guitar or autoharp, strumming on the beat. Use resonator bells, glockenspiel, or xylophone to provide contrasting timbres for the chord changes.

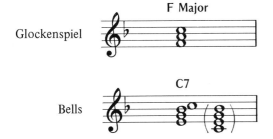

Creating a second vocal part

2. Select several members of the class to sing this second part using melodic syllables or "loo" on each note.

do   mi   sol   mi   ti,   re   sol   ti,
1   3   5   3   7   2   5   7

do   mi   sol   mi   fa   fa   mi   mi
1   3   5   3   4   4   3   3

3. Durational syllables practice:

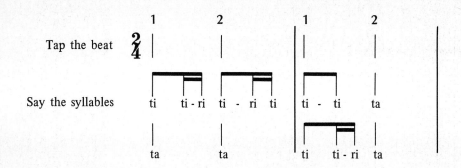

Tap the beat

Say the syllables   ti   ti - ri   ti - ri   ti   ti - ti   ta

ta   ta   ti   ti - ri   ta

4. Assist the class in developing movement accompaniments that express the question-answer form of the song.

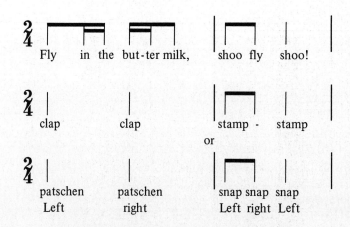

Fly   in the but-ter milk,   shoo fly   shoo!

clap   clap   stamp - stamp

or

patschen   patschen   snap snap snap
Left   right   Left right Left

A verse to chant and play

The Grand Old Duke of York

[1]"O the Grand old Duke of York, He
[2]Had ten thousand men; He
[3]Marched them up a great high hill, And he
[4]Marched them down again!

[5]When they were up, they were up, And
[6]When they were down, they were down, And
[7]When they were only halfway up, They were
[8]Neither up nor down!

From verse to rhythmic notation

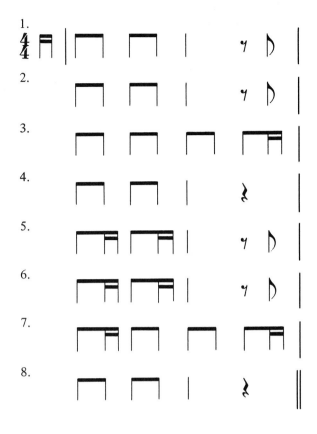

POLLY WOLLY DOODLE

fay   For I'm   going   to   Loui - si - an - a   for   to

see   my   Su - si - an - nah   Sing - ing   Pol - ly   Wol - ly   Doo - dle   all   the   day!

Chord changes on Orff instruments

Teaching Suggestions

1. Have the students play their own accompaniment on Orff instruments using these patterns:

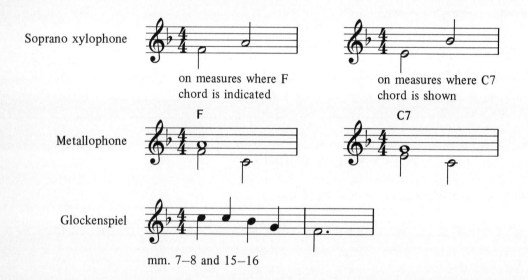

Soprano xylophone

on measures where F chord is indicated

on measures where C7 chord is shown

Metallophone

F

C7

Glockenspiel

mm. 7–8 and 15–16

2. Divide the class into two groups to sing or play recorders on the refrain. Add this part to the song:

Refrain
Fare thee well . . .

Arranged by R. Herrold

Fare thee well,   Fare thee well,   Fare thee well my   fay,

I   am   go - ing   to   Su - san - nah,   Pol - ly   wol - ly   all   the   day.

BEAUTIFUL BROWN EYES

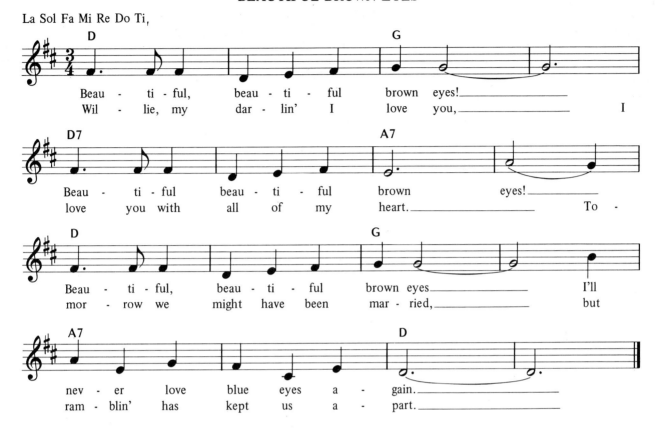

La Sol Fa Mi Re Do Ti,

Beau - ti - ful, beau - ti - ful brown eyes!
Wil - lie, my dar - lin' I love you, I

Beau - ti - ful beau - ti - ful brown eyes!
love you with all of my heart. To -

Beau - ti - ful, beau - ti - ful brown eyes I'll
mor - row we might have been mar - ried, but

nev - er love blue eyes a - gain.
ram - blin' has kept us a - part.

Teaching Suggestions

1. Ask the students to sing the syllables as they follow your hand signs.

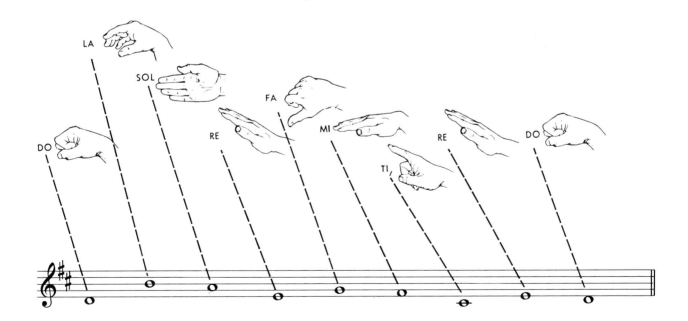

An unaccompanied two-part song   2. Divide the class into two groups to sing unaccompanied. Add this part to the song.

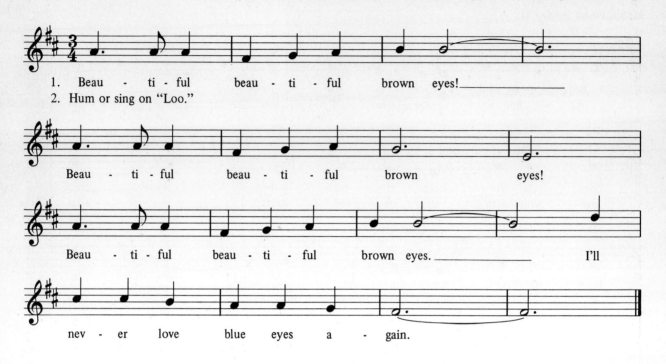

1. Beau - ti - ful   beau - ti - ful   brown   eyes!_____
2. Hum or sing on "Loo."

Beau - ti - ful   beau - ti - ful   brown   eyes!

Beau - ti - ful   beau - ti - ful   brown eyes._____   I'll

nev - er   love   blue   eyes   a - gain.

THE FROG AND THE MOUSE

La Sol Fa Mi Re Do Ti, La,

Solo There was   a frog lived in   a well,   Group Whip - see did - dle dee   dan - dy O!
Solo There was   a mouse lived in   a mill,

This   frog he would a - woo - ing ride, With sword and pis - tol   by   his side, With a

har - um scar - um did - dle dum dar - um, Whip - see did - dle dee   dan - dy O!

Teacher Preparation

1. Study the D natural minor scale associated with this song and its relative major, F.

la, ti, do re mi fa sol la   do re mi fa sol la ti do'

2. Practice singing the first line of this song using the syllables and numbers of the D natural minor scale.

la,	la,	do	mi	do	fa	re	do	la	la,	la,	ti,	do	ti,	la,	la,
1,	1,	3	5	3	6	4	3	(8/1)	1,	1,	2,	3	2,	1,	1,

3. Lead your methods class in this echo-clapping exercise. Sway left-right on the beats while you clap, and ask the class to follow you.

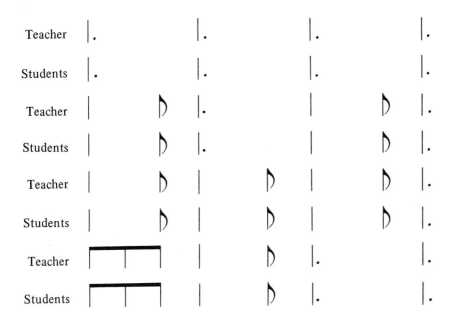

Teaching Suggestion

Ask a student to play woodblocks on the nonsense words, "Whipsee diddle dee dandy O!" Glockenspiel or bells can be played on the repeated melodic figure in measures 5–8 on D, C, and A.

A WORRIED MAN

Mi Re Do Ti, La, Sol,

It takes a wor-ried man to sing a wor-ried song, It

takes a wor-ried man to sing a wor-ried song, It

takes   a wor - ried man   to   sing   a wor - ried song, I'm wor - ried

(Count 1   2   3   4)
now,_____ but I   won't be wor - ried long.

Teaching Suggestion

Harmonizing in thirds and sixths   Ask the students to read this second part to harmonize in thirds and sixths.

It   takes   a wor - ried man   to   sing   a wor - ried song,   it

takes a wor - ried man   to   sing a wor-ried song,   it takes a wor - ried man   to

sing a wor-ried song. I'm wor - ried   now,   but I   won't be wor-ried long.

BINGO

Fa Mi Re Do Ti, La, Sol,

There was a farm - er   had a dog, And Bin - go was his   name - o.

B - I - N - G - O,   B - I - N - G - O,

B - I - N - G - O, and Bin - go was his   name - o.

Teaching Suggestion

Ask the class to work with you on this inner hearing activity. After they sing the song through, they can develop five successive verses by dropping one letter from BINGO in each verse. First, sing B-I-N-G and "think the O," then B-I-N and "think the G and the O," etc., until the class is resting on measures 5–9 and part of 10. For a variation on this idea, assign an instrument to each letter of BINGO and ask students to play on the letters that are dropped by the singers.

AIN'T GONNA GRIEVE MY LORD NO MORE

grieve   my   Lord   no   more._____   *f* I   ain't   gon-na
grieve   my   Lord   no   more._____   *p* I   ain't   gon-na

grieve   my   Lord   no   more,   I   ain't   gon-na   grieve   my   Lord   no
grieve   my   Lord   no   more,   I   ain't   gon-na   grieve   my   Lord   no

more,   Ain't   gon-na   grieve   my   Lord   no   more._____
more,   Ain't   gon-na   grieve   my   Lord   no   more._____

Teaching Suggestions

Try these schemes in performing the call-and-response, or *antiphonal,* section of this song.

call	response
a. solo vocalist	a. group of vocalists
b. group of vocalists	b. glockenspiel, bells, or xylophones on melody
c. group of vocalists	c. autoharps or bells on chords played on the beats
d. group singing lyrics	d. second group responding with improvised movement on rhythm of lyrics
e. group humming melody and clapping rhythm of melody simultaneously	e. second group imitating first group
f. group singing lyrics	f. second group singing lyrics on chord tones

Oh, you can't   get   to   heav'n _____

SHOO FLY, DON'T BOTHER ME

Sol Fa Mi Re Do Ti, Sol,

Shoo fly,   don't   both-er   me,   Shoo   fly,   don't   both-er   me,

Teacher Preparation

Practice this piano accompaniment for the song.

BOW BELINDA

Sol Fa Mi Re Do Ti, Sol,

1. Bow, bow, bow Belinda; Bow, bow, bow Belinda;
Bow, bow, bow Belinda; Won't you be my darling?

2. Right hand around, Belinda, *etc.*

3. Left hand around, Belinda, *etc.*

4. Both hands around, Belinda, *etc.*

5. Shake your foot, Belinda, *etc.*

6. Join right hands, Belinda, *etc.*

7. Join left hands, Belinda, *etc.*

8. Promenade, Belinda, *etc.*

9. Circle, all, Belinda, *etc.*

Teaching Suggestions

1. Provide variety in this short dance-song with a second part which can be added to selected verses, and chords **I** and **V₇** in F Major hummed or sung with syllables.

Arranged by R. Herrold

Bow, bow, bow Be-lin-da (repeat _ _ _ _ _ _ _ _ _ _ _ _)

(repeat _ _ _ _ _ _ _ _ _ _ _ _) Won't you be my dar-ling?

Hum hum hum hum hum hum hum hum

hum hum hum hum hum hum hum

% indicates that the performer should repeat the previous measure

2. Assist the students in preparing an Orff accompaniment for the song.

Xylophone

Metallophone

CLEMENTINE

Sol Fa Mi Re Do Ti, Sol,

1. In a cav - ern, in a can - yon, Ex - ca - vat - ing for a mine, Dwelt a
miner, for - ty - nin - er, And his daugh - ter Clem - en - tine.

Chorus

Oh, my dar - ling, Oh, my dar - ling, Oh, my dar - ling Clem-en - tine! You are
lost and gone for - ev - er, Dread - ful sor - ry, Clem - en - tine!

2. Light she was, and like a fairy,
   And her shoes were number nine,
   Herring boxes without topses,
   Sandals were for Clementine.

3. Drove she ducklings to the water
   Every morning just at nine,
   Hit her foot against a splinter,
   Fell into the foaming brine.

4. Ruby lips above the water
   Blowing bubbles soft and fine;
   As for me, I was no swimmer
   And I lost my Clementine.

5. How I missed her, how I missed her,
   How I missed my Clementine,
   Then I kissed her little sister,
   And forgot dear Clementine.

Teacher Preparation

Review the rhythm of the dotted eighth-sixteenth note pattern.

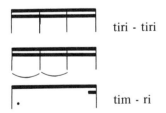

tiri - tiri

tim - ri

Teaching Suggestions

1. Prepare the class for the rhythm of the song by having them mirror your motions as soon as they are aware of the pattern.

etc.

(patschen) Clap

2. Ask class members to play an *arpeggiated* (broken chord) bell accompaniment for the song. This type of accompaniment works well when the chord changes are always on the first beats of the measures.

An arpeggiated bell accompaniment

Bells or recorders

DOWN IN THE VALLEY

Sol Fa Mi Re Do Ti, Sol,

1. Down in the val - ley, the val - ley so low, Hang your head o - ver, hear the winds blow, Hear the winds blow, dear, hear the winds blow, Hang your head o - ver, hear the winds blow.

2. If you don't love me, love whom you please,
   Throw your arms 'round me, give my heart ease,
   Give my heart ease, dear, give my heart ease,
   Throw your arms 'round me, give my heart ease.

3. Throw your arms 'round me, before it's too late,
   Throw your arms 'round me, feel my heart break.
   Feel my heart break, dear, feel my heart break,
   Throw your arms 'round me, feel my heart break.

4. If you don't love me, none else will do,
   My heart is breaking, dear, just for you.
   Breaking for you, dear, breaking for you,
   My heart is breaking, dear, just for you.

5. Writing this letter, containing three lines,
   Answer my question: Will you be mine?
   Will you be mine, dear, will you be mine,
   Answer my question: Will you be mine?

6. Build me a castle forty feet high,
   So's I can see him as he goes by.
   As he goes by, dear, as he goes by,
   So's I can see him as he goes by.

7. Down in the valley, the mocking bird wings,
   Telling my story, here's what he sings:
   Roses love sunshine, violets love dew,
   Angels in heaven know I love you.

8. Know I love you, dear, know I love you,
   Angels in heaven know I love you.
   Know I love you, dear, know I love you,
   Angels in heaven know I love you.

Teaching Suggestions

1. Introduce the students to the $\frac{9}{8}$ time signature with mirror movement exercises which emphasize the triple meter of the song. Ask the class to imitate your movements as soon as they are aware of the patterns.

The $\frac{9}{8}$ time signature

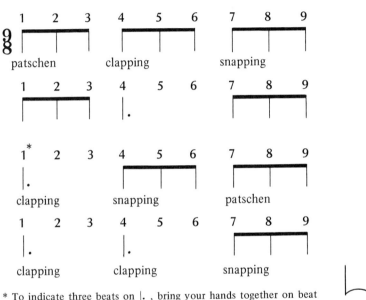

* To indicate three beats on |. , bring your hands together on beat one and move them together on beats two and three.

2. Ask the class how they would like to arrange this song to provide variety within the many verses. They may experiment with dynamic changes, have soloists or small groups perform some of the verses, use autoharp, guitar, bell, or piano accompaniments with two chords, and sing some of the verses unaccompanied.

3. Have the students read this second part for the song. It may be sung or played on bells or recorders.

Arranged by R. Herrold

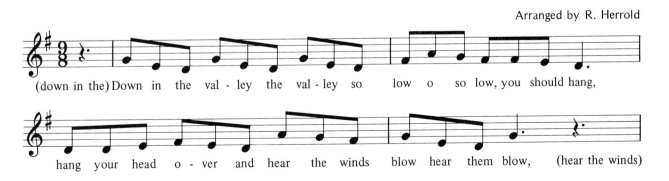

Hear the winds blow my dear hear the winds blow in the val - ley be - low,

Hang your head o - ver and hear the winds blow, hear them blow.

RED RIVER VALLEY

Sol Fa Mi Re Do Ti, La, Sol,

From this val - ley they say you are go - ing, _____ We will

miss your bright eyes and sweet smile, For they say you are tak - ing the

sun - shine, _____ That has bright - ened our path - way a - while.

Chorus

Come and sit by my side if you love me, _____ Do not

has - ten to bid me a - dieu, But re - mem - ber the Red Riv - er

val - ley, _____ and the boy that has loved you so true.

Teacher Preparation

Piano and guitar accompaniments in F Major

Practice playing the 3-chord accompaniment for this song on the autoharp, piano, and guitar.

Piano Chords

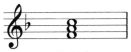

F Major

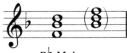

B♭ Major

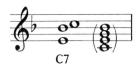

C7

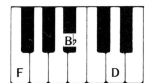

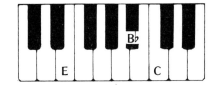

Guitar Chords

F Major

B♭ Major

C7

Accompaniment: for autoharp, guitar, or bells

4/4 𝄾

		F				
	B♭			
	F			
	C7			

	F			
	B♭			
	F		C7	
	F			:‖

Teaching Suggestion

Harmonizing in thirds   Teach this second part for the chorus of the song by rote.

Come and sit by my side if you love me,_____ Do not has‑ten to bid me a‑dieu, But re‑mem‑ber the Red Riv‑er val‑ley,_____ and the boy that has loved you so true.

PICK A BALE O' COTTON

Sol Fa Mi Do Ti, La, Sol,

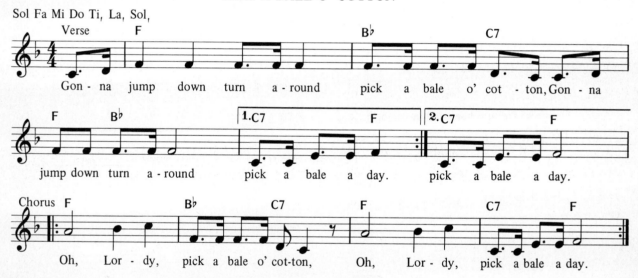

Gon‑na jump down turn a‑round pick a bale o' cot‑ton, Gon‑na jump down turn a‑round pick a bale a day. pick a bale a day.

Oh, Lor‑dy, pick a bale o' cot‑ton, Oh, Lor‑dy, pick a bale a day.

Teacher Preparation

Practice this accompaniment for the song. Remember to keep your left hand in place, for two adjacent keys provide the notes needed for the bass part.

Fine

D.C. al Fine

Teaching Suggestions

1. This is an action song. Have the class act out the lyrics of the verse as they stand in place. On "Oh, Lordy," ask them to stand on tiptoe and reach up with both arms. On "pick-a-bale-o'-cotton" ask them to bend at the waist and act out the lyrics.

2. Ask a student to play this part on resonator bells or glockenspiel.   Acting out lyrics

THE ALLEE-ALLEE O

Sol Fa Mi Re Do Ti, La, Sol,

From *Singing Games and Play-Party Games* by Richard Chase, Copyright 1967 by Dover Publications, Inc. New York. Reprinted through permission of the publisher.

Teacher Preparation

1. Write out on a chalkboard staff the notes in F major that are used in this song. Give your methods class the pitch of *do,* or 1, and have them sing syllables or numbers of the notes as you point to them.

2. Practice an autoharp accompaniment for the song strumming on the first beat of each measure. In the two places where a fermata ⌒ is located, strum slowly across the strings to extend the duration of the beat.

Teaching Suggestions

1. Assign a student to play the glockenspiel or bells on the last four measures, "Hi! Ding-dong-day!"

2. Assign bell players to play on the beats of "Allee, allee O".

3. Substitute names of rivers or oceans for "Allee, allee O". Try "Mississippi O" or "Caribbean O" or "Chattahoochee O".

PAW-PAW PATCH

La Sol Fa Mi Re Do Ti, Sol,

3. Come on boys, let's go find her,
   Come on boys, let's go find her,
   Come on boys, let's go find her,
   Way down yonder in the paw-paw patch.

Teaching Suggestions

1. Assist the students in transposing the song from G Major to F Major.

Transposing from G Major to F
Major

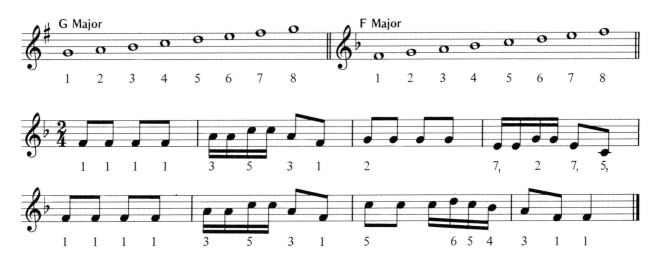

2. Ask the students which lines of the song are alike or different. The form of the song is ABAC.

3. *Parallel Line Dance:* Boys form one line, girls another, with partners facing one another. On the words ''Where, oh where,'' girl 1 skips behind the girls' line, then around the boys' line and back to her place. When ''come on boys'' is sung, the same girl repeats her skipping, now with the line of boys following her. These dancers return to their original positions at the end of the verse. On verse 3 the dancers turn to face the ''top'' of the set and the boys follow boy 1 around to the left while the girls follow girl 1 around to the right.

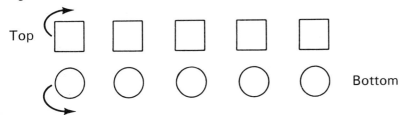

Lois Choksy, *The Kodaly Context: Creating an Environment for Musical Learning,*
© 1981, p. 229. Reprinted by permission of Prentice-Hall, Inc. Englewood Cliffs, N.J.

Boy 1 and girl 1 form an arch at the bottom of the set and the remaining dancers skip through the arch and back into the original lines. Couple 2 is in place at the top and the game is repeated.

JIMMY CRACK CORN

La Sol Fa Mi Re Do Ti, La, Sol,

U.S. Folk Song

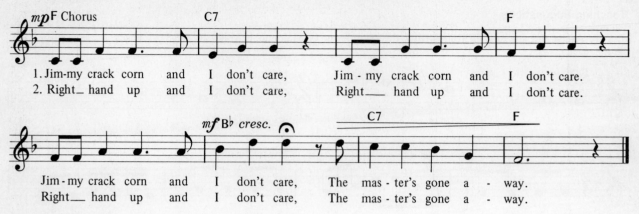

1. Jim-my crack corn   and   I don't care,   Jim-my crack corn   and   I don't care.
2. Right— hand up   and   I don't care,   Right— hand up   and   I don't care.

Jim-my crack corn   and   I don't care,   The mas-ter's gone a - way.
Right— hand up   and   I don't care,   The mas-ter's gone a - way.

3. Left hand up, *etc.*

4. Both hands up, *etc.*

5. Jimmy crack corn, *etc.*

Teaching Suggestions

The fermata

1. Make use of contrasting styles for the verse and the chorus. The verse is effectively presented in a free, dramatic manner with emphasis on the fermatas indicated for "bright," "night," and "say." The verse may be accompanied with a single strum per measure on autoharp or guitar, and sung by a soloist. The refrain is sung by the class in a steady rhythm, with attention to the upward contour of the melody and its relationship to the dynamic markings.

2. Ask the class to create some ostinato patterns to perform on rhythm instruments to accompany the refrain. They may want to include these:

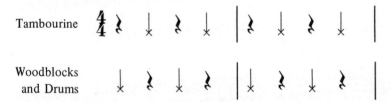

Reading mixed and irregular meters

Tap out the following exercises, keeping the beat steady as you move from $\frac{4}{4}$ to $\frac{3}{4}$ to $\frac{2}{4}$.

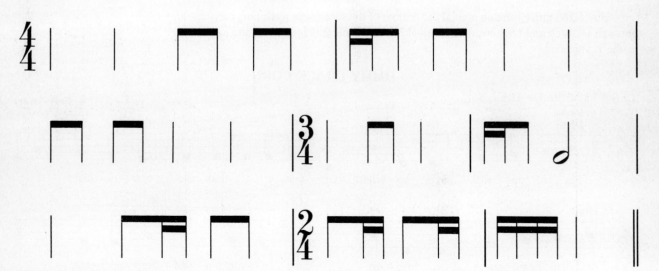

Play this exercise in an irregular meter. Keep the beats steady and follow the accents carefully, as they assist you in grouping the 5-beat patterns.

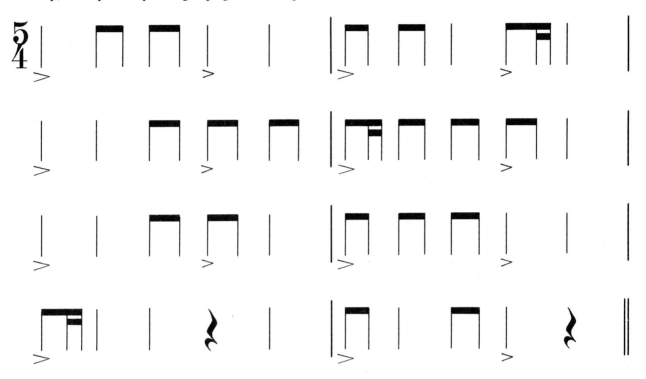

I'M ON MY WAY

La Sol Fa Mi Re Do Ti, La, Sol,

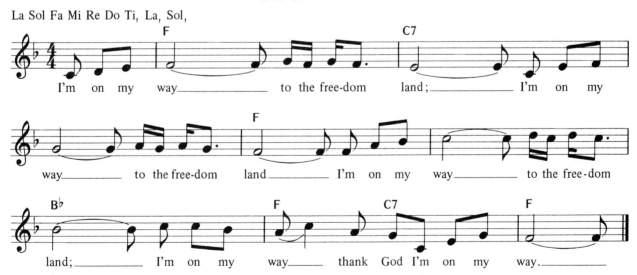

I'm on my way_____ to the free-dom land;_____ I'm on my way_____ to the free-dom land_____ I'm on my way_____ to the free-dom land;_____ I'm on my way_____ thank God I'm on my way._____

2. I'll ask my friends to come with me; *(repeat three times)*
   I'm on my way; thank God! I'm on my way.

3. If they won't go, then I'll go alone: *(repeat three times)*
   I'm on my way; thank God! I'm on my way.

4. I'm on my way and I won't turn back; *(repeat three times)*
   I'm on my way; thank God! I'm on my way.

Teacher Preparation

Study this illustrated plan for teaching students to read the rhythm of this spiritual. Practice tapping the subdivided beats and counting aloud. Finally, tap the beats and say the lyrics in correct rhythm. This rhythm is repeated twice.

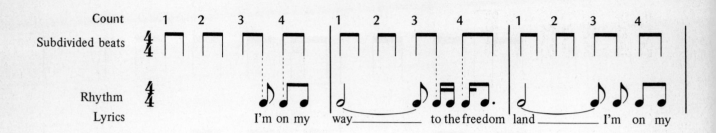

Teaching Suggestions

1. Ask the students to sing the song in antiphonal style with half the students performing the response, or echo, parts.

call: I'm on my way _____ to the freedom land _____

response: I'm on my way _____ to the freedom land

2. Work with your class to create contrasting presentations for the four stanzas of this song. Employ solo voices, groups of vocalists, bodily movement, and rhythm and melodic instruments.

SWEET BETSY FROM PIKE

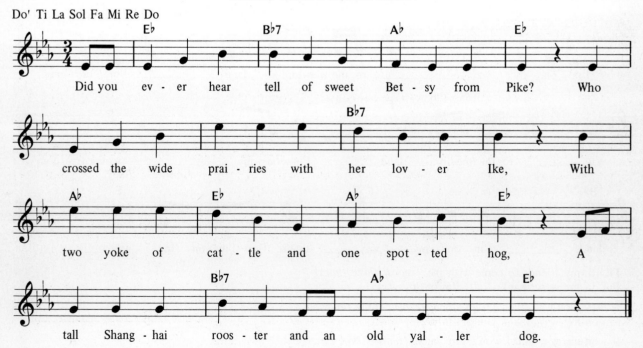

Teacher Preparation

1. Locate the notes needed to create a major scale beginning on E♭. Remember to place half steps between 3–4 and 7–8. Include all letters of the musical alphabet (E F G A B C D E). Which notes must be changed or altered to create the half steps? Write the scale and put in the key signature to show which notes are affected.

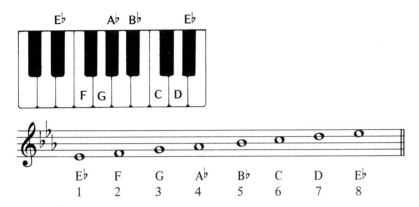

2. On your piano find the **I, IV,** and **V₇** chords in E♭ Major.

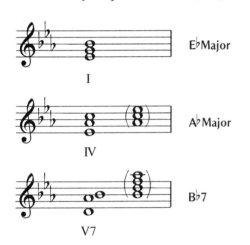

Locating chord tones in E♭ Major

3. Practice this piano accompaniment in E flat Major for "Sweet Betsy."

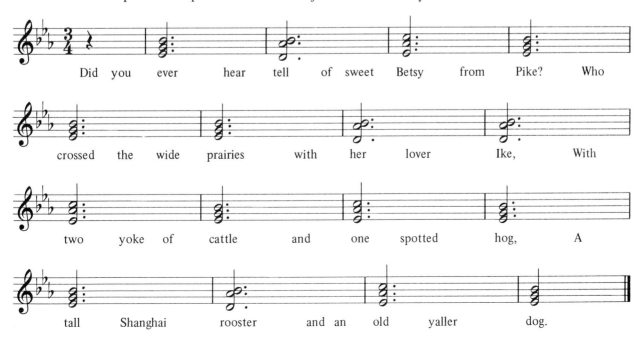

Teaching Suggestion

Ask the class to suggest rhythm and melodic instruments which could be associated with the lyrics of the song and performed on the corresponding notes or rhythmic patterns. They might want to try a scheme like this:

Glockenspiel:	Betsy from Pike F E♭ E♭ E♭
Resonator bells:	her lover Ike D B♭ B♭ B♭
Cowbells:	two yoke of cattle
Xylophone:	one spotted hog A♭ B♭ B♭ C
Autoharp (one strum on E♭ Maj.):	tall, Shanghai rooster
Woodblocks	Old yaller dog.

THE TAILOR AND THE MOUSE

3. The tailor thought his mouse would die,
   Hi diddle umkum feedle.
   He baked him in an apple pie,
   Hi diddle umkum feedle.

4. The pie was cut, the mouse ran out,
   Hi diddle umkum feedle.
   The tailor followed him all about,
   Hi diddle umkum feedle.

Teacher Preparation

1. Sing and play at the keyboard the E minor scale associated with this song.

2. Now write the same scale and raise the seventh degree by one half step. This alteration is not accommodated by the key signature and requires the use of an *accidental*. This change creates the *harmonic minor* scale. Note that the D♯ is used in the B Major chord of the accompaniment.

la,   ti,   do   re   mi   fa   si   la   E minor   B Major

Note that the raised *sol* is named *si*. The hand sign for *si* is

Si and its hand sign

Teaching Suggestions

1. Ask the class to create a bodily movement accompaniment for the verse, and a contrasting one for the chorus.

2. Ask the class to find the nonsense words in the lyrics ("Hi diddle umkum feedle"). Is the melody the same or different when these words are repeated? Ask the students to play the rhythm of the nonsense words on sticks or melodic percussion instruments.

THE JACKFISH

Sol Mi Re Do Ti, La, Sol, Mi,

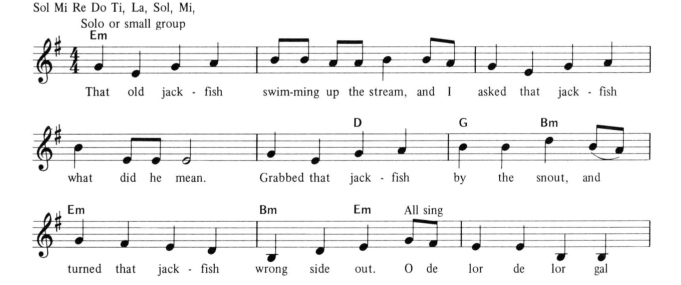

Reprinted from *Jim Along Josie*, collected by Cecil Sharp. Used by permission of Novello & Co. Ltd., London.

Teaching Suggestions

1. Have a soloist or small group sing the first eight measures unaccompanied. Remember to give the starting pitch before they begin. Add autoharps on the last 4 measures, strumming on beats 1 and 3 in $\frac{4}{4}$.

2. Add woodblocks on beats 3 and 4 for the first 7 measures. Use a triangle on beat 1 in measures 9–12 along with the woodblocks.

OLD KING COLE

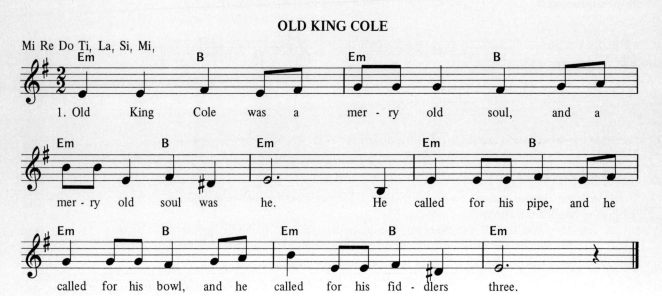

Mi Re Do Ti, La, Si, Mi,

1. Old King Cole was a mer-ry old soul, and a mer-ry old soul was he. He called for his pipe, and he called for his bowl, and he called for his fid-dlers three.

2. Every fiddler, he played a fine tune,
And a very fine tune played he;
Twee dum tweedle dum went the King's fiddlers three,
Tweedle dum, tweedle dum, tweedle dee.

3. Old King Cole was a merry old soul,
And a merry old soul was he;
He called for his pipe and he called for his bowl,
And he called for his pipers three.

4. Every piper, he had a fine pipe,
And a very fine pipe had he;
Too too toodle too went the King's pipers three,
Toodle too, toodle too, toodle dee.

Teaching Suggestions

1. Have the students perform their own accompaniment on Orff instruments using these patterns.

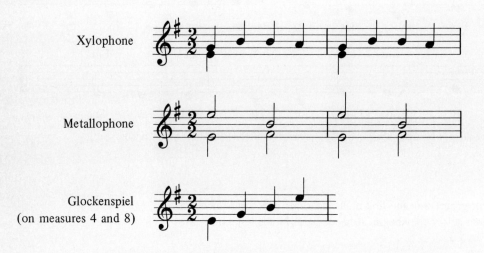

Xylophone

Metallophone

Glockenspiel
(on measures 4 and 8)

2. Ask the students to use an autoharp or piano accompaniment with two chords on some of the verses to give variety to their performance. An introduction can be created by having an autoharp strummed while a woodblock plays the rhythm of the lyrics on the last 4 measures of the song. This idea can also be used to create interludes between the verses and a coda, or ending, when the song is finished.

PAT WORKS ON THE RAILWAY

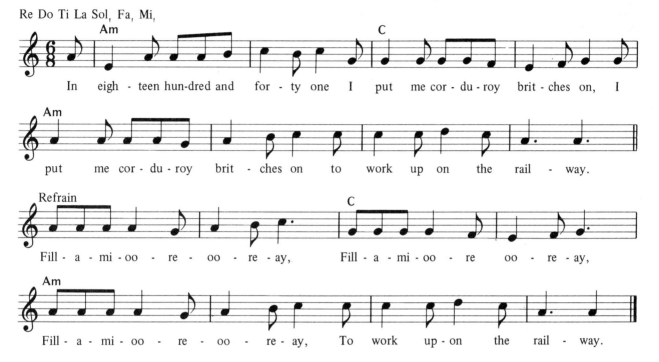

Teaching Suggestions

1. Assist the class in writing the A natural minor scale associated with this song. Review with them that minor scales begin on *la* and that *do* indicates the name of the relative major scale, here, C Major.

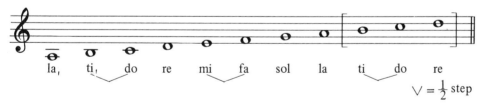

The A natural minor scale

2. Rhythm accompaniment with bodily movement:

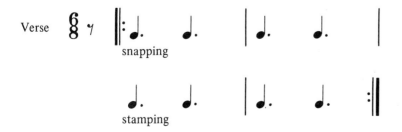

Refrain

patschen

clapping

YANKEE DOODLE

Fa Mi Re Do Ti, La, Sol, Fa, Mi,

Yank - ee Doo - dle   went to town a - rid - ing on a   po - ny,

Stuck a feath - er   in his cap and   called it mac - a - ro - ni.

Yan - kee Doo - dle   keep it up,   Yan - kee Doo - dle   Dan - dy,

Mind your mu - sic   and your step and   with the girls be   hand - y.

Teaching Suggestions

1. Introduce the *triplet* in an echo movement exercise.

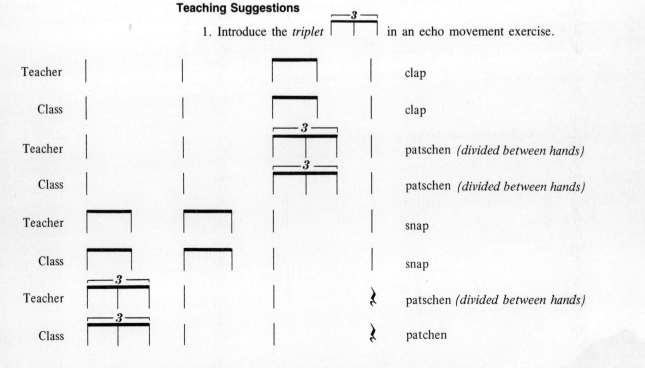

Teacher				clap
Class				clap
Teacher				patschen *(divided between hands)*
Class				patschen *(divided between hands)*
Teacher				snap
Class				snap
Teacher				patschen *(divided between hands)*
Class				patchen

The durational syllables for the triplet are helpful and enable students to evenly divide the beat into three equal parts.

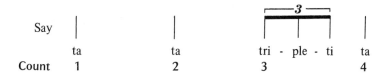

2. Ask several class members to play this introduction and rhythm accompaniment for "Yankee Doodle". Use hand drums, rhythm sticks, and woodblocks.   The tri-ple-ti pattern

Arranged by R. Herrold

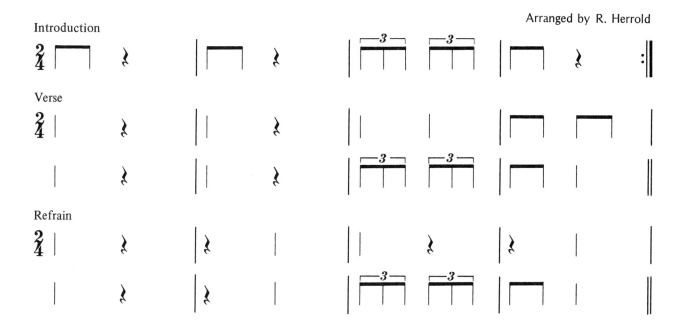

JOHNNY HAS GONE FOR A SOLDIER

Do' Ti La Si Sol Mi Re Do

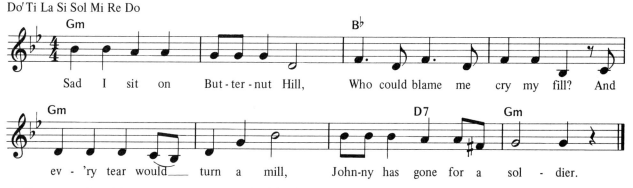

Sad I sit on But-ter-nut Hill, Who could blame me cry my fill? And ev-'ry tear would turn a mill, John-ny has gone for a sol-dier.

2. Me o my, I loved him so.
Broke my heart to see him go.
And only time will heal my woe,
Johnny has gone for a soldier.

3. I'd sell my clock, I'd sell my reel,
Likewise I'd sell my spinning wheel,
To buy my love a sword of steel
Johnny has gone for a soldier.

Teaching Suggestions

1. Assist the class in writing the harmonic minor scale associated with this song. Remember that *sol* is raised one-half step in measure 7 and is called *si*. The hand sign for *si* is

la,　ti,　do　re　mi　fa　si　la　ti　do'

Ask the class how this minor scale differs from the natural minor.

2. Ask several class members to play this second part for the song on their recorders.

Accompanying a song with recorders

DRILL YE TARRIERS, DRILL

Do' Ti La Sol Mi Re Do Ti, La,

Well,　ev-'ry morn-ing at　se-ven o' clock There were twen-ty tar-ri-ers a

work-in' at the rock,　and the　boss comes a-round and he　says "Keep still, and

come down heav-y on the　cast　i-ron drill." and　Drill　ye　Tar-riers,

Drill!　And　drill, ye tar-riers　drill!　For it's　work all　day for the

su - gar in your tay, Down be-hind the rail · way, and drill ye tar - ri - ers

drill! And blast, and fire, And blast, and fire.

Teacher Preparation

1. Study the C natural minor scale and its relative major, E♭.

C minor

la, ti, do re mi fa sol la | ti do'

E♭ Major

do re mi fa sol la ti do

2. Locate the three chords you will need to accompany this song on a piano. Practice playing the chords on beats 1 and 3 of each measure.

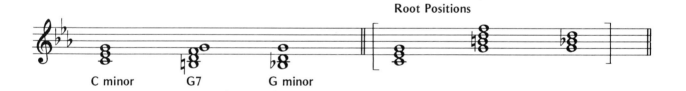

Root Positions

C minor   G7   G minor

Teaching Suggestions

When the class has learned to sing this song with confidence, ask the students to help you develop appropriate instrumental ostinato patterns that reflect the origins of the music. Tell them that this is a nineteenth century song of the immigrant Irish railroad workers. "Tay" means tea here, and "tarriers" may refer to the beards of the workers which resembled terrier coats. Remind the class that since the work of the men was monotonous and hard labor, metallic sounds and repetitive rhythms are best suited to the lyrics. Measure 9 is the beginning of the chorus, and your class should make some change in the style of the accompaniment at this point to mark the principal divisions of the song.

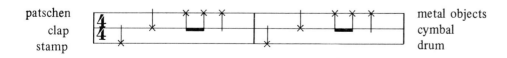

patschen   metal objects
clap   cymbal
stamp   drum

OLD JOE CLARKE

Ta La Sol Fa Mi Re Do Sol,

1.Round and round,   old Joe Clarke,   round and round I   say,

Round and round,   old Joe Clarke,   I ain't got long to   stay.   *Fine*

Old Joe Clarke he   had a house,   Six - teen stor - ies   high,

Ev - 'ry sto - ry   in that house was   full of chick - en   pie.   *D.C. al Fine*

2. Rock-a-rock, old Joe Clarke,
Rock-a-rock, I'm gone;
Rock-a-rock, Old Joe Clarke, and
Goodbye, Susan Brown.

Old Joe Clarke he had a dog as
Blind as he could be;
Chased a redbug 'round a stump and a
Coon into the tree.

Teacher Preparation

1. Modes are eight tone scales with specific patterns of whole and half steps. Major and minor scales were among the church modes that were the basis of European music in past centuries. Although major keys dominate American folk music, minor keys and the dorian and mixolydian modes have an important influence.

Play these modes on the piano.

Dorian mode D - D   Mixolydian mode G - G

2. Study the scale associated with "Old Joe Clarke." Note that the seventh degree is flatted and creates a half step between 6 and 7. The altered note is called *ta*. This arrangement of scale degrees is referred to as the *mixolydian mode* and is frequently found in U.S. folk music, particularly that of the southeastern region.

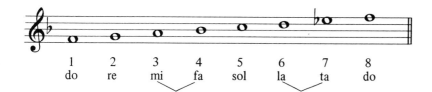

1	2	3	4	5	6	7	8
do	re	mi	fa	sol	la	ta	do

3. Practice the hand sign for *ta* as it is used in the context of the song.

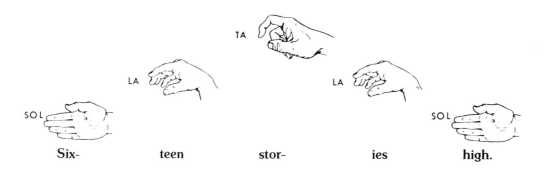

Six-   teen   stor-   ies   high.

HOLD ON

La Si Sol Mi Re Do La,

When you plow, don't lose your track.___ Can't plow straight and keep a-

look - in' back.___ Keep your hand on___that plow,___

Hold on, hold on, hold on. Hold on, hold on,

Bet-ter keep your hand right on___ that plow,___ Hold on, hold on, hold on.

3. Keep on plowin' and don't you tire,
   Ev'ry row goes higher and higher.
   Keep your hand on that plow,
   Hold on, hold on, hold on.
   (Refrain)

4. If that plow stays in your hand,
   Head you straight for the promised land.
   Keep your hand on that plow,
   Hold on, hold on, hold on.
   (Refrain)

Teacher Preparation

This song can be accompanied with two chords, D minor and A_7, with the A_7 appearing in only one measure. Practice this pattern, keeping a steady beat in $\frac{4}{4}$.

Teaching Suggestions

Ask the class to perform their own accompaniment on the Orff instruments using these patterns. At the refrain use autoharps on A_7 and D minor for two measures. Then resume the accompaniment with the mallet instruments.

WRITING PRACTICE: Minor Scales

1. Write the natural minor scales beginning with the notes given. Put in the key signatures. Use a keyboard to locate the half steps.

2. Write the harmonic minor scales beginning with the notes given. Put in the key signatures. Use a keyboard to locate the half steps.

WADE IN THE WATER

La Si Mi Re Do La, Si, Mi,

Wade____ in the wa-ter,____ Wade____ in the wa-ter lit-tle child-ren.

Wade____ in the wa-ter,____ God's gon-na trou-ble the wa-ter.____

Mem-ber one thing and it's cer-tain-ly sure____ Wade____ in the wa-ter____

Judg-ment's com-in' and I don't__know____ Wade____ in the wa-ter.____

2. Upon the mountain, Jehovah, he spoke
Wade in the water
Out of his mouth came fire and smoke.
Wade in the water.

3. Down in the valley, down on my knees
Wade in the water
Asking my Lord to hear me, please.
Wade in the water.

Teacher Preparation

1. Develop a piano accompaniment using the D minor and A_7 chords similar to the one shown for "Hold On." Practice as your methods class sings, keeping a steady beat in $\frac{4}{4}$.

2. Develop a bodily movement accompaniment that features a different motion for each of the four beats. Then repeat the pattern for each measure of the song.

Part 5

Microcomputers in the
Elementary Music Class

The key to understanding not only the future of teaching computers but also much of the future impact of computers on society lies in one fact: miniaturized, super cheap, highly reliable computer technology will open up markets of staggering size—at first in Westernized societies and later in the Third World. . . . And one of the biggest untapped markets in the world is the application of computers to education.

Christopher Evans*

The advent of the inexpensive microcomputer is now providing the potential for individualized instruction at all levels of the educational system. Teachers just entering the profession, as well as those of longstanding experience, will find that each year their students are more sophisticated about the new technology and increasingly receptive to its presence in the classroom. The preparatory curriculum for teachers in all disciplines must, therefore, include at least fundamental information about computers, how technology can assist in the teaching and learning process, and a review and criticism of existing courseware appropriate for the various subjects and levels. For teacher-training institutions to ignore the advancing technology is to place the rapid commercialization of educational software in the hands of marketing specialists who may not take pedagogical techniques into consideration in designing programs for classroom and home educational use.

A Brief History of Teaching Machines

Probably the first systematic attempt to implement a psychological theory of learning with a mechanism was made by Maria Montessori soon after she initiated her first *Casa dei Bambini* in Rome in 1907. Her didactic apparatus anticipated some of the concepts found

Today's Education, Spring 1982

later in programmed instruction. One of her devices, for example, consisted of a block of wood with ten holes of different diameters and ten wooden cylinders to fit the holes. This device was dependent on the activity of the young learner for its use. It was necessarily self-corrective with immediate feedback, and the child could proceed at her own pace.[2]

Sidney Pressey, at the 1925 meetings of the American Psychological Association, exhibited a device which anticipated more modern teaching machines. This device gave the student a choice of four possible answers to a question in a window and four keys which the student used to select the answer. If the student thought the second answer was correct, he pressed the second key; if he was right, the next question was turned up. If the second was not the right answer, the initial question remained in the window and the learner persisted until he found the right one. Meanwhile a record of all tries was kept automatically.[3]

B. F. Skinner, the Harvard psychologist whose experiments with pigeons during World War II led to the theories of response-reward psychology, found that pigeons could learn elaborate movements and even color discriminations when the complex steps of learning were broken into smaller units and successes were immediately reinforced. Skinner's theory touches on nearly all the main ideas of the programmed learning and the teaching machine movements that gained popularity in the 1950s. He found that reinforcement of correct behavior is a necessary part of the learning process and studied the classroom teacher as a source of that reinforcement. He arrived at the conclusion that it is usually physically impossible for a teacher to provide every student with individual reinforcement each time it is appropriate and necessary. He found that a tutor, on the other hand, interacting directly with one student, can provide the guidance necessary to allow the student to arrive at a correct response. A tutor can adapt to the student's progress by further elaboration of ideas, repetition, and changes in the pace of study.[4]

Skinner's research led him to develop an autoinstructional technique. This method consisted of direct interactions between a student and a special program of material presented by a mechanical device that came to be known as a teaching machine. Whereas the earlier attempt by Pressey focused on testing students upon completion of a regular course of study, Skinner's machine was the first to function as a teacher of students who have had no previous contact with the subject matter. Skinner reported in 1958 that the effect of his machine was surprisingly like that of a private tutor: (1) there was constant interchange between program and student, (2) the machine insisted that a given point be understood before the student moved on, (3) the machine presented only that material for which the student was ready, and (4) the machine reinforced the student for every correct response.[5] The computer-assisted instructional systems now available are capable of much more.

Basic Features of Computer-Assisted Instruction (CAI)

Whereas the main contribution of the earliest teaching machines was the individualized pacing of the tutorlike presentations and reinforcements, the microcomputer has an infinite flexibility for teaching purposes. The range of tasks it can perform is limited only by the imagination and pedagogical skill of the authors who write for it. In addition to providing tutorials and drill-and-practice exercises in sequence, the microcomputer can be programmed to

[2]Maria Montessori, *The Montessori Method,* tr. by A. E. George. (Philadelphia: J. B. Lippincott Co., 1912), p. 190.

[3]Sidney L. Pressey, "Autoinstruction: Perspectives, Problems, Potentials" in *Theories of Learning and Instruction,* Sixty-third Yearbook of the National Society for the Study of Education (Chicago: University of Chicago Press, 1964), pp. 355, 356.

[4]William A. Deterline, *An Introduction to Programmed Instruction* (Englewood Cliffs, N.J.: Prentice-Hall, Inc., 1962), p. 11.

[5]B. F. Skinner, "Teaching Machines," *Science,* CSSVIII (1958), p. 971.

1. Address the student by name.
2. Advance the student through an instructional program according to predetermined standards of success. For example, the student will remain in a unit until she reaches a 90 percent level of accuracy in her responses.
3. Keep track of student responses for the teacher.
4. Keep individual and class profiles of student progress.
5. Help teachers diagnose areas of student weakness by providing statistical information regarding the incidence of incorrect response to a given problem.
6. Provide help through *branching:* when a student makes an error he receives more feedback than just ''wrong.'' He is branched to information designed to let him know why and how his response was in error before he is returned to the main lesson.
7. Change the role of the teacher to that of a mentor or coach whose primary role in the CAI classroom is to find appropriate programs for individual children and to encourage them as they master the material.

Sometimes when teachers first consider using a computer in their classroom, they are overtaken by the all-too-common fear of being replaced by a machine. That apprehension is quickly allayed when the teacher realizes that the computer alone can never achieve the effectiveness of a human teacher. The two in combination, however, create a powerful teaching force which gives good teaching the potential for great teaching.

Fundamentals of Microcomputers

The computer is an electronic device which does its work by following precisely written sets of instructions called programs. All computers have several components in common.

Central Processing Unit (CPU): Performs the fundamental computations specified in the computer's built-in program.

Memory: Stores programs and data. There are two types, 1) random-access (temporary) memory, referred to as RAM and 2) read-only (permanent) memory, referred to as ROM.

Clock: Determines the order in which the computer performs its tasks.

Interfaces: Connect the computer with other devices that make it more flexible.

> *Terminal Interface:* Allows the computer to communicate with a video screen and keyboard. Additional interfaces permit the user to interact through the computer with other video media.
>
> *Disk Interface* (*Controller*): Provides quick storage and retrieval of data and programs.
>
> *Cassette Interface:* Provides audiocassette storage of programs and data.
>
> *Synthesizer Interface:* Allows the computer to generate sounds for music composition or CAI.
>
> *Speech Interface:* Allows the computer to talk and receive human speech (to functionally ''understand'').
>
> *Printer Interface:* Allows the computer to command a printer to print lists of programs or results of programs.
>
> *MODEM:* Provides the capability for the computer to interact with other computers through the telephone.

Bus: A set of plugs or receptacles into which peripheral hardware may be installed to enhance the computer's capabilities. A bus is also used internally to transfer data among areas in the system.

Chip: The tiny electronic component upon which a microcomputer's major capabilities are concentrated.

Floppy Disk: The most cost-effective, high-speed, random-access data device. The disk resembles a 45 rpm record in size and is very thin (thus floppy). It has two sides coated with a magnetic oxide surface similar to that of audiotape. Data are recorded in circles, and a disk may hold from 50,000–300,000 or more characters of data on one side. A program can be loaded from a disk to a computer in 5–30 seconds.

Program: Required list of instructions for the computer. These instructions may be written in several kinds of computer "languages".

Machine Language: The built-in actions a computer can perform.

Assembly Language: A language that people can understand, although it is difficult to learn. The computer translates this language into machine language.

High-Level Language (BASIC, Pascal, FORTRAN, COBOL): An English-like language designed to make it relatively convenient for an author or programmer to prepare a list of instructions for a computer. The computer also translates this language into machine language.

Computer-Assisted Instruction in Music

Perhaps no other discipline included in the elementary school curriculum has been as positively affected by CAI as music education. Microcomputers have proved to be particularly suited for music instruction because music notation can be displayed with computer graphics, many microcomputers can generate specific pitches, and a variety of synthesizers and keyboard interfaces are available to enhance the computer's capability to perform music and function as an instrument. Several leading university music departments have pioneered developments in CAI music applications that are now deemed appropriate for elementary and secondary students.

A microcomputer in the elementary classroom can serve as a learning station for individualized instruction in several subjects. Lessons in music that are available include drill and practice in sol-fa, naming notes, relating speech patterns to rhythmic notation, aural practice in learning rhythmic notation, keyboard drills for practice in locating notes on the piano, and key signature identification. Programs are available for elementary music composition that allow a student to program a computer with information about a composition which may be stored, retrieved, and "performed" by the micro.

Sample Drill-and-Practice Programs in Music CAI: Rhythm Reader and Sol-Fa (Tutor)

An elementary music program called "Rhythm Reader" is designed for microcomputer drill-and-practice in reading rhythm notation. Three patterns are displayed in graphics and the student listens as the computer "plays" one of the patterns. She then selects the corresponding notation from the three choices. An important feature of this program is its capacity to generate the patterns on one pitch or randomly selected pitches within an octave range. The latter assists students in working with rhythmic perception within a melodic configuration. This program allows students to hear an example as many times as they wish before selecting an answer, and they may select the tempo of the patterns' performance. The program is intended to *complement class work* in reading.

Here is an example of a drill-and-practice program:

graphics display:

instruction to student:	Which one do you hear? Type 1, 2, or 3, and press the *Return* key. Or type "R" to hear the pattern repeated.
sound:	Computer plays pattern 2.
student input:	Student types "2, *Return*."
computer response:	"You're off to a good start!"
graphics display:	

	Which one do you hear? Type 1, 2, or 3. Type "R" to hear the pattern repeated.
sound:	The computer plays pattern 1.
student input:	Student types "R" to hear example again.
computer response:	Pattern is repeated.
student input:	Student types "2."
computer response:	I'll play the pattern again. Tap or clap with me as I play. (*pattern is repeated—student taps with computer*) Now try again.
graphics display and sound:	Sequence is repeated.

The student continues to receive instruction in the first unit of Rhythm Reader until he exits to a new program, or until his time runs out. Unit 1 includes duple meter exercises and durational values of quarter, eighth, and sixteenth notes and rests. As he progresses through consecutive Rhythm Reader units he will receive extra-class work in triple, compound, and irregular meters.

The drill-and-practice lessons in hearing and reading melodic syllables begin with the intervals found in the natural chants and songs of children, *sol-mi* and *sol-la-mi*. The computer displays rhythm patterns and plays melodic intervals in the rhythm indicated. The student identifies the melodic intervals she hears from three possible answers. Again, this program is intended to reinforce class work in reading, and should not be used by children until they have been introduced to syllables work in class.

Graphics Display:

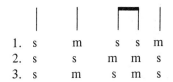

1. s   m   s s m
2. s   s   m m s
3. s   m   s m s

	Which pattern do you hear? Type 1, 2, or 3. Type R to hear the pattern again.
Sound:	*sol-sol-mi-mi-sol*
Student Input:	Student types "2."
Computer Response:	Good!

Graphics Display:

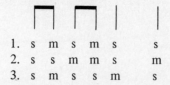

```
1.  s   m   s   m   s       s
2.  s   s   m   m   s       m
3.  s   m   s   s   m       s
```

The student is guided through graded units of interactive drill-and-practice until he has completed the pentatonic lessons.

Doremi and Arnold: Two Ear-Training Games (MicroMusic)

The "Doremi" games are intended to augment class work in the study of sight-singing, and are appropriate for students who have been introduced to the major scale. This series teaches students to identify by sound the individual degrees of a major scale. The program procedes in this way:

1. As the computer performs a major scale, the student listens and may hear it as many times as desired.
2. Once familiar with the tones of the scale, the student instructs the computer to play a single tone. The tone is sounded.
3. The student identifies the scale degree and may choose to answer by typing the scale numbers (1, 2, 3, 4, etc.) or syllables (*do, re,* etc.)
4. The computer tells the student if he or she is right or not. If correct, the student is congratulated and moved on to identify the next tone. If the answer is wrong, the computer plays the tone selected, then the correct tone. Finally, the computer shows how the correct tone fits into the scale.
5. Upon attainment of 90 percent accuracy in identifying one scale tone at a time, the student may go on to Doremi 2—a program that presents two scale degrees in sequence. There are four programs, and the student progresses through them as fast as his or her increased musical ability will allow.

"Arnold" is an ear-training program which gives students out-of-class practice in developing melodic memory skills. There are five levels of difficulty and nineteen melodies at each level. The student can progress sequentially, or skip around for review work or more challenging patterns. The programs are presented in this way:

1. First, Arnold allows the student to hear a scale as many times as desired.
2. Then, if the student is in Level 1, a tone is sounded. (There are up to four tones in succession in Level 5).
3. The student identifies the tone(s) he or she has heard by scale degree numbers (1, 2, 3, 4) or syllables (*do, re, mi*). In this program only three typewriter keys are needed to respond: the → key, the ← key, and the space bar. A display on the screen presents either the syllables or the numbers. The student moves the cursor up and down the scale with the arrow keys and presses the space bar to enter his response.
4. If the response is incorrect, it is displayed and sounded, then followed by the correct melody. This gives the student a chance to compare his mistakes with the correct melody.
5. The student is asked to enter the melody again.
6. Arnold adds tones to an ever-increasing melody until the student has successfully identified all its tones.

At any time while working with Arnold, the student can request to see a report of his progress. Arnold keeps track of:

name
date
level
number of exercises completed
number of errors
percentage score

Arnold will store up to 101 student entries for the teacher's records.

How to Evaluate Music Courseware

Music teachers who select courseware for their students must have guidelines for its evaluation. The mere appearance of a staff, clef, and notes accompanied by computer-generated sound in an educational program is indeed awesome for the first-time viewer and listener. However, close scrutiny is needed before purchases are made. Good courseware has some common characteristics.

1. *Adequate documentation*. There must be sufficient information for the instructor regarding the loading of disks, peripherals required for operation, and how much instruction the students will need before they work at computer terminals. The instructor needs to be aware of the monitoring required once the student is seated at the terminal. It should be minimal.
2. *Instructions for the student should be brief*. At the beginning of the program, students should be given examples to try that are exactly like the problems they will be given during the instruction that follows. They should not be given paragraphs of confusing jargon.
3. *Accurate music notation and pitches must be used*. Be wary of programs that present notation in unrealistic shapes and disproportionate sizes of noteheads, stems, and beams. These can be very confusing to the beginning viewer, whereas they are easily translated by the seasoned musician. Pitches should be on-target for *all* CAI music programs. (If a classroom teacher who is selecting software is unsure of pitch accuracy in a program, he or she should consult a professional musician for assistance.)
4. *The program must be "crashproof."* The instructor should touch keys on the computer that are not among those designated for making responses. (Children, of course, will do this!) The program should not stop, nor should there be any interference when this occurs.
5. *The capabilities of the computer should be utilized*. A CAI program should provide more than "page-turning" information and style which a student can obtain just as well from a textbook. The feedback to the students should be helpful, allowing them to compare their results, if incorrect, with the correct ones. If the programs are "electronic flashcards" they should be advertised as such. Sometimes such programs are entirely appropriate for drill-and-practice. The teacher needs to know what the program is intended to accomplish.
6. *Feedback should be related to the accomplishment*. Feedback for correct responses should not always be in the superlative, such as "You're the greatest!" "Super!" and "What a whiz!" These should be reserved for significant achievement or improvement.
7. *Exit possibilities*. The student should be able to stop, get out of the program and back to the selection "menu", and enter into a new program at any time. (The menu lists all programs available to the user.) The directions for exiting should be simple and appear in the program's instructions at the beginning of the lesson.

Programming a Microcomputer

Elementary teachers may be motivated to learn computer programming as they develop curriculum and instructional materials. However, since programming is time-consuming and in a constant state of change, they might prefer to work with professional programmers to develop their own materials or critique available software to determine its suitability for their classrooms. In either case, some experience with beginning programming is helpful, for such a background equips teachers with knowledge about what computers can be expected to accomplish in the educational process.

Teachers interested in programming should keep in mind two important steps that are too often overlooked: field testing and modification. Successful CAI programs have been through several periods of testing and modification to take out "bugs" in the programs. The ratio of development hours to student hours is approximately 200 to 1—a challenging figure for a would-be CAI developer. This ratio includes instructional design, programming, testing, and debugging.

Programming a Sample Lesson in PILOT

PILOT is a simple, easy-to-understand programming language originally developed by Dr. John Starkweather at the University of California, San Francisco. PILOT stands for *Programmed Inquiry for Learning or Teaching* and was designed to enable teachers to write programs for their students. PILOT was originally conceived as a tool to make writing conversational programs easy, and due to the pioneering work of Dr. Dean Brown at Stanford Research Institute's Education Laboratory, has proved to be a good language for teaching programming to children. Although PILOT was at first designed for text output only, the Atari Company PILOT has incorporated Turtle Graphics, a concept developed by Dr. Seymour Papert and the LOGO group at the Massachusetts Institute of Technology. Turtle Graphics enables the programmer to draw pictures and symbols in a program. This capability, along with PILOT's ability to generate sounds (specific pitches), makes Atari PILOT a useful language for music teachers and their students.

Try these short programming lessons in PILOT to get started. You will need an Atari 400/800 computer, a PILOT cartridge, and a color monitor.

T Type

```
10   R: Major or Minor Keys in a Folk Song
20   T: Is "The Frog and the Mouse" in a major or minor key?
30   A:
40   M: minor, miner, min.
50   TY: Yes, the notes at the beginning of the song form a minor triad on D,F,A ("There was
         a frog.")
60   TN: No, if the song were in a major key the notes at the beginning would form a major
         triad (D, F♯, A).
70   E:
RUN
```

Interpretation of Program I

line command	instructions to computer
10 R:	The R: (REMARK) command is a title or reminder that lets you identify your program. The R: will be ignored by the computer when your program is executed by your RUN command.
20 T:	The T: (TEXT) command tells the computer to display what you type.
30 A:	The A: (ACCEPT) command tells the computer to wait for the user to type in an answer or information on the computer keyboard.
40 M:	The M: (MATCH) command matches the answer entered by a user during an A: command with the answers anticipated by the program's author. This allows the programmer to allow for abbreviations and possible spelling mistakes in student responses. M: automatically creates a YES (Y) or NO (N) condition.
50 TY:	The TY: (TEXT if YES). The author can write a positive response to the user's answer here. If the response is incorrect, TY: will be skipped and the program will execute TN:.

60   *TN:*   The TN:(TEXT if NO) will be shown if the user's answer is incorrect.

70   *E:*   The E: (END) marks the end of your program. RUN tells the computer to exe-cute the program currently in memory.

II. type

5 *R:*	The C Major Scale in Quarter Notes
10 *SO:13*	
20 *PA:64*	
30 *SO:15*	
40 *PA:64*	
50 *SO:17*	
60 *PA:64*	
70 *SO:18*	
80 *PA:64*	
90 *SO:20*	
100 *PA:64*	
110 *SO:22*	
120 *PA:64*	
130 *SO:24*	
140 *PA:64*	
150 *SO:25*	
160 *SO:0*	

Interpretation of Program II

command   *instructions to computer*

   SO: The SO: (SOUND) command allows you to create musical tones on your computer and to program up to four tones to play at the same time. The tones you can play in PILOT range from SO: 1 to SO: 31. SO: 1 produces a tone equal to the C one octave below middle C on the piano. SO: 31 generates the tone F sharp, one octave above middle C. SO: O turns the sound off.

SO:

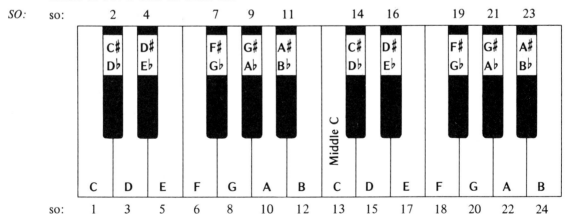

   PA: The SO: and PA: (PAUSE) commands are used together to create music. The PAUSE values for musical notes are based on PA: 60 which has a duration of 1 sec-ond and PA: 30 which pauses ½ second.

        PA: 16   sixteenth note
        PA: 32   eighth note
        PA: 64   quarter note
        PA: 128 half note
        PA: 256 whole note

Sources of Elementary Music CAI Programs

1. Computer Applications Tomorrow
   P. O. Box 605
   Birmingham, Michigan 48012

   This company offers music instructional programs for use with Apple II, Atari and TRS-80.

2. Control Data Corporation
   8100 34th Ave., S.
   Minneapolis, Minnesota 55440

   CDC has much elementary music courseware for the PLATO system. Games and drill-and-practice programs are available for teaching note reading, key signatures, intervals, keyboard-note relationships and melodic and rhythmic structures. Plans are underway for conversion of PLATO courseware to microcomputer disks.

3. Educational Audio Visual, Inc.
   Pleasantville, New York 10570

   a. *Music* for Atari 400/800

   Drill-and-practice programs in music fundamentals including terms and notation, rhythm and intervals, scales and chords.

   b. *Musical Computers* for Apple II+, TRS-80 model III, and Atari 800.

   Programs for the beginning music student, covering note reading on treble and bass clefs, rhythm practice, keyboard-note correlation, signs and symbols, and tempo definitions.

   c. *Ear Challenger* for Apple II+

   This program provides a drill on tonal memory through a series of seven randomly played notes that correspond to color graphics on the screen. The game offers four levels of increasing difficulty ranging from 3 to 7 pitches and from 5 to 37 sequences of notes.

4. Electronic Courseware Systems
   PO Box 2374
   Station A
   Champaign, Illinois 61820

   "Elements of Music" on instructional software covers pitch names, pitches on the keyboard, and key signatures.

5. MicroMusic and Temporal Acuity Products
   1535 121st Ave., S. E.
   Bellevue, Washington 98005

   Elementary software for the Apple II includes among many programs

   a. DOREMI (augments class work in the development of sight-singing)

   b. Arnold (for development of melodic memory skills)

   c. Music Symbols

   d. Standard Instrument Names

   e. General Music Terms

   f. Name That Tune (ear-training game)

   g. Pitch Identification Drills

6. Notable Software
   P. O. Box 1556-ME
   Philadelphia, Pennsylvania 19105

   Music software includes a game called "Note Trespassing."

7. Tutor, Co.
   P. O. Box 41092
   San Jose, California 95160

   MusicTutor includes elementary music software for the Apple II which is also appropriate for classroom teacher preparation.

   a. Sol-Fa Drills

   b. Speech Patterns (derived from U.S.A. folk songs)

   c. Rhythm Reader

Organizations for Educational Uses of Computers

1. Apple for the Teacher
   5848 Riddio St.
   Citrus Heights, California 95610

   An organization which has the National Computer Assisted Instruction Library for the Apple computer. Software is contributed from all over the world. Its newsletter reviews educational software and provides information on educational computing grants and research.

2. Association for the Development of Computer-Based Instructional Systems (ADCIS)
   Bond Hall
   Western Washington University
   Computer Center
   Bellingham, Washington 98225

   Members include elementary and secondary school systems, colleges, businesses and governmental agencies. Its purpose is to increase communication between developers and users.

3. Boston Computer Society
   Educational Resource Exchange
   Three Center Plaza
   Boston, Massachusetts 02108

   The Exchange provides information on funding teacher training, equipment selection and software availability.

4. Computer Music Association
   911 22nd Ave., S. #181
   Minneapolis, Minnesota 55404

   This organization was formed to help develop computer applications to music and provides members with a newsletter on computer hardware and software in the field.

5. Computer-Using Educators
   Independence High School
   1776 Educational Park Dr.
   San Jose, California 95133

   Organized in conjunction with San Jose State University, this group has members around the country. It publishes a bimonthly newsletter, holds two major conferences per year, and maintains a software library.

6. Courseware, Inc.
   10075 Carroll Canyon Rd.
   San Diego, California 92131

   A company that designs materials to suit the needs of its clients.

7. Educator's Hot Line
   Vital Information, Inc.
   913-384-3860

   A group that answers questions about software and publishes a general software directory.

8. Microcomputer Education Applications Network
   256 North Washington St.
   Falls Church, Virginia 22046

   An organization that helps educators develop and sell software and assists local districts and state education agencies.

9. MicroSIFT
   Northwest Regional Educational Laboratory
   300 6th Ave., S.W.
   Portland, Oregon 97204

   A clearinghouse for software and teacher information. Provides materials and services for educational uses at K-12 level.

10. Minnesota Educational Computing Consortium (MECC)
    2520 Broadway Dr.
    St. Paul, Minnesota 55113

    This is the largest educational computing network in the world, serving all public education institutions in Minnesota. MECC develops and sells software for Apple and publishes a newsletter.

11. National Consortium for Computer-Based Music Instruction (NCCBMI)
    Music Education Division
    School of Music
    University of Illinois
    Urbana, Illinois 61801

    A subgroup of ADCIS (see 2) that provides a focus for the exchange of ideas among developers and users of computer-based systems for music instruction, and maintains a library of music courseware. Consultation for new users of computer-based music instruction is provided. Members receive a newsletter, yearbook, and the *Journal of Computer-Based Instruction*.

12. Texas Computer Education Association
    7131 Midbury
    Dallas, Texas 75230

    Provides information on current trends in K-12 computer education, works to improve teacher training, supports a software exchange, and publishes a quarterly newsletter.

Sources of Recordings for Classroom Listening

Bowmar Records, Inc.
4563 Colorado Blvd.
Los Angeles, California 90039
(for *Meet the Instruments* and *Bowmar Orchestral Library*)

Capitol Records
Educational Dept.
Capitol Tower
1750 North Vine St.
Hollywood, California 90028
(for Capitol and Angel Records Educational Catalog)

Columbia Records, Inc.
Educational Dept.
799 Seventh Ave.
New York, New York 10019

Educational Records Sales
157 Chambers St.
New York, New York 10007

RCA Records
P. O. Box 1999
Indianapolis, Indiana 46291
(for *Adventures in Listening*)

RCA Victor Educational Sales
155 E. 24th St.
New York, New York 10010
(for RCA Victor Basic Record Library)

Scholastic Records
906 Sylvan Ave.
Englewood Cliffs, New Jersey 07632

Sesame Street Records
1 Lincoln Plaza
New York, New York 10023

Glossary

Accent = > (handwritten)

accelerando   Increasing the speed of the beat.

alla breve (¢)   A tempo mark indicating $\frac{2}{2}$ meter instead of $\frac{4}{4}$; quick duple time with the half note rather than the quarter note as the beat.

anacrusis   An incomplete measure which occurs before the first complete measure of a musical work.

arpeggio   Tones of a chord that are sung or played in succession rather than simultaneously.

autoharp   A folk instrument of Bavarian origin used for accompanying melodies; played by depressing buttons which damp all the strings except those required for a specific chord.

bass clef (𝄢: **F clef**)   A symbol that indicates the position of F on the staff; used for lower tones.

beat   The basic pulse of music.

blue note   The name applied in jazz music to the third and seventh degrees of the scale, which are used both natural and flatted and frequently with a deliberately sliding intonation in between.

bordun   The first and fifth degrees of the scale sounded simultaneously in a repeated rhythmic figure as an accompaniment for a chant or song.

canon   A musical work in which all the parts have the same melody but start at different times. *(Round)* (handwritten)

clef   From the Latin *clavin,* meaning key. A sign placed at the beginning of the staff to indicate a specific pitch.

coda   A section at the end of a piece that brings it to a close.

compound meter   A meter, in which the subdivision of the beat is in three, as in $\frac{6}{8}$, $\frac{9}{8}$, and $\frac{12}{8}$.

crescendo (⟨)   Gradually becoming louder.

Curwen hand signs   Hand positions which use a specific shape to represent each of the syllables of the musical scale.

D.C. al Fine (***Da Capo al Fine***)   From the beginning to the sign *Fine.*

decrescendo (>) Gradually becoming softer.

diatonic scale A scale consisting of whole and half steps.

duple meter A meter in which the beat units are grouped by two, such as $\frac{2}{2}$, $\frac{2}{4}$, $\frac{2}{8}$, and $\frac{2}{16}$

durational syllables Syllables which represent the actual length of note values and which are used to facilitate the reading of rhythm as isolated from pitch.

TA TiТ

fermata (⌒) A hold or pause.

Fine Italian term meaning ''the end.''

flat (♭) A symbol indicating that a pitch is to be lowered a half step.

forte (*f*) Loud, strong.

fortissimo (*ff*) Very loud.

glissando Sliding toward a tone instead of attacking it directly.

glockenspiel A percussion instrument consisting of graduated metal bars which are struck with mallets. Produces a bright, ringing sound.

half step The smallest interval written in notation; a semitone.

improvisation Musical performance that is spontaneous, without aid of memorization or notation.

interval The distance between two tones. The name is determined by counting all pitch names within that distance. Examples:

4th

6th

inversion A chord in which the root does not appear as the lowest tone.

key signature The sharps or flats at the beginning of the staff indicating the altered notes that form the scale or key of the music.

legato A connected, smooth manner.

major scale The scale used frequently in Western music in which the pattern of whole and half steps is:

$$1 \quad 2 \quad 3 \underset{\text{½ step}}{\smile} 4 \quad 5 \quad 6 \quad 7 \underset{\text{½ step}}{\smile} 8$$

measure repeat sign (✗) instructs performer to repeat preceding measure

metallophone A percussion instrument consisting of graduated bars of metal which are struck with mallets. Produces a sustained tone of mellow quality.

meter The grouping of beats by accents in groups of two, three, four, five, six, seven, nine, or twelve.

minor scale A type of scale characterized by its half step between the second and third degrees.

mixolydian Refers to a scale with half steps between three–four and six–seven.

natural sign (♮) A symbol that cancels a sharp or flat which appears earlier in the score.

octave An interval in which two pitches show the same letter name; i.e. A-A, with one pitch at twice the frequency of the other.

Orff instrumentarium An ensemble of instruments designed by composer-pedagogue, Carl Orff. These are intended to give young players a means for creating music through improvisation. They include glockenspiel, metallophones, xylophones, recorders, stringed and percussion instruments.

ostinato A repeated melodic or rhythmic figure. May be chanted, sung, played on instruments, or performed with bodily movement to create an accompaniment.

patschen Tapping the right hand on the right knee and the left hand on the left knee, either simultaneously or consecutively.

pentatonic scale A five-tone scale which is built on the major or minor scales.
Major: *do re mi sol la*
Minor: *la do re mi sol*

phrase A musical segment with an identifiable beginning and ending. May be compared to a sentence in speech.

Marcato – Deliberate-marked-accented

pianissimo (*pp*)   Very soft.

piano (*p*)   Soft. The name "piano" as applied to the instrument comes from the Italian *Gravicembalo con piano e forte*, meaning a keyed instrument with both soft and loud tones.

pizzicato (*pizz.*)   The plucking of a string on a stringed instrument.

relative major   A major key that has the same key signature as its related minor key; a scale which begins on the third step of the relative minor scale.

relative minor   A minor key that has the same key signature as its related major key; a scale which begins on the sixth step of its relative major scale.

repeat signs (:‖:)   Symbols used to indicate that the music between the signs should be repeated.

rhythm   The organization of sound in time.

ritardando (rit.)   Gradually delaying the beats.

rondo   A musical form in which one section recurs, i.e. A   B   A   C   A.

root   The tone on which a chord or triad is built.

rubato   A style of performing in which one note may be extended at the expense of another for purposes of expression.

sharp (♯)   A symbol indicating that a pitch is to be raised a half step.

staccato   Detached short sounds; opposite of legato.

staff   A series of horizontal equidistant lines upon which the pitches and rhythms are indicated.

syncopation   Displacement of the accent from a strong to a weak beat.

transposition   Changing a piece of music from one key to another.

treble clef ($\mathcal{G}$: G clef)   The symbol indicating the position of G on the staff; used for higher register notation.

triple meter   Regular grouping of beat units by three ($\frac{3}{2}$, $\frac{3}{4}$, $\frac{3}{8}$)

upbeat   (*see* **anacrusis**)

whole step   An interval made up of two consecutive half steps.

xylophone   from Greek *xylos* (wood) and *phone* (sound). A percussion instrument consisting of graduated bars of hardwood which are struck with mallets.

Time Signature

A Selected Bibliography

Books on Music

ABRAMSON, ROBERT M. *Rhythm Games for Perception and Cognition*. New York: Music and Movement Press, 1973.

ADAM, JENO. *Growing in Music with Movable Do*. Highland Park: Kossuth Foundation, 1971.

CHOKSY, LOIS. *The Kodaly Context*. Englewood Cliffs, NJ: Prentice-Hall, Inc., 1974.

——. *The Kodaly Method*. Englewood Cliffs, NJ: Prentice-Hall, Inc., 1974.

ERDEI, PETER AND KATALIN KOMLOS. *One Hundred Fifty American Folk Songs to Sing, Read and Play*. New York: Boosey and Hawkes, 1974.

FINDLAY, ELSA. *Rhythm and Movement: Applications of Dalcroze Eurhythmics*. Evanston, Ill: Summy-Birchard, 1971.

GELL, HEATHER. *Music, Movement and the Young Child*. Sydney: Australian Publishing Co., 1973.

HALL, DOREEN AND ARNOLD WALTER. English adaptation of *Music for Children* by Carl Orff and Gunild Keetman, Volume I: Pentatonic. Mainz: B. Schott's Sohne.

JACQUES-DALCROZE, EMILE. *Rhythm, Music and Education*. New York: Dalcroze School of Music, Revised Edition, 1967.

KEETMAN, GUNILD. *Elementaria*. London: Schott, 1974.

KODALY, ZOLTAN. *The Selected Writings of Zoltan Kodaly*. London: Boosey and Hawkes, Ltd., 1974.

LANDIS, BETH AND POLLY CARDER. *The Eclectic Curriculum in American Music Education: Contributions of Dalcroze, Kodaly and Orff*. Music Educators National Conference, 1972.

LANGSTAFF, JOHN AND NANCY. *Jim Along Josie: A Collection of Folk Songs and Singing Games for Young Children*. New York: Harcourt Brace Jovanovich, Inc., 1970.

MARQUIS, MARGARET H. *Songs for All Seasons and Rhymes Without Reasons*. New York: Marks Music Corp., 1968.

MONSOUR, SALLY, MARILYN COHEN AND PATRICIA LINDEN. *Rhythm in Music and Dance for Children*. Belmont, CA: Wadsworth Publishing Co., 1966.

NASH, GRACE. *Creative Approaches to Child Development with Music, Language and Movement*. Port Washington, NY: Alfred Publishing Co., 1974.

RICHARDS, MARY HELEN. *Threshold to Music*. Belmont, CA: Fearon Publishers, 1970.

SEEGER, RUTH CRAWFORD. *American Folk Songs for Children*. Garden City, NY: Doubleday and Co., 1950.

TEACHING STAFF OF KODALY MUSICAL TRAINING INSTITUTE. *Teaching Music at Beginning Levels Through the Kodaly Concept* (2 volumes). Wellesley: Kodaly Musical Training Institute, 1973.

WORTHING, MICHELLE GRATIS. *Elements of Music*. Dubuque, IA: Wm. C. Brown Co., 1978.

Books and Articles on Computers

STUDENT PILOT REFERENCE GUIDE. Atari, Inc. Sunnyvale, California, 94086.

DOERR, CHRISTINE. *Microcomputers and the Three R's: A Guide for Teachers*. Rochelle Park, New Jersey. Hayden Book Co., Inc., 1979.

EVANS, CHRISTOPHER, FRANZ FREDERICK AND OTHERS. "Microcomputers in the Classroom," *Today's Education*. The Journal of the National Education Association. April-May, 1982.

HERROLD, REBECCA. *Computer-Assisted Instruction: A Study of Student Performance in a CAI Ear-Training Program*. (Unpublished doctoral dissertation) Stanford University, 1974.

HOFSTETTER, FRED T. "Music Dream Machines: New Realities for Computer Based Music Instruction." *Creative Computing*. March-April, 1977, pp. 50–54.

—— "Instructional Design and Curricular Impact of Computer Based Music Education." *Educational Technology*, April 1978, pp. 50–53.

NAISBITT, JOHN. *Megatrends*. New York: Warner Books, 1982.

PAPERT, SEYMOUR. *Mindstorms: Children, Computers and Powerful Ideas*. New York: Basic Books, 1980.

PETERS, G. DAVID AND JOHN EDDINS. "Applications of Computers to Music Pedagogy, Analysis and Research: A Selected Bibliography." *Journal of Computer-Based Instruction,* August and November 1978, pp. 41–44.

TAYLOR, R. P. (ED.) *The Computer in the School: Tutor, Tool, Tutee*. New York: Teacher's College Press, 1980.

Song Indexes

Songs Grouped by Melodic Syllables

Alphabetical Index of Songs

Index of Verses